ESTATE LEDGER

1. The Front Garden
2. The Great Lawn
3. The Italian Terrace Garden
4. Three Frog Fountain
5. Citrus Terrace
6. Neptune Terrace
7. Three-Tiered Italian Fountain
8. Coral Tree
9. Lower Tennis Court
10. Swimming Pool
11. Pool Pavilion
12. The Display Rose Garden
13. Upper Tennis Court
14. Aviary in Palm Forest
15. The Orchid Greenhouse
16. Male Staff Quarters
17. The Kitchen Terrace
18. Main Residence
19. The Palm Forest
20. The Palm Terrace with Pond
21. Cutting Rose Garden

Beverly Hills' First Estate

Beverly Hills' First Estate

The House and Gardens *of* Virginia & Harry Robinson

Timothy Lindsay, Marcella Ruble, and Evelyn Carlson

Edited by Maralee Beck and Jamie Wolf

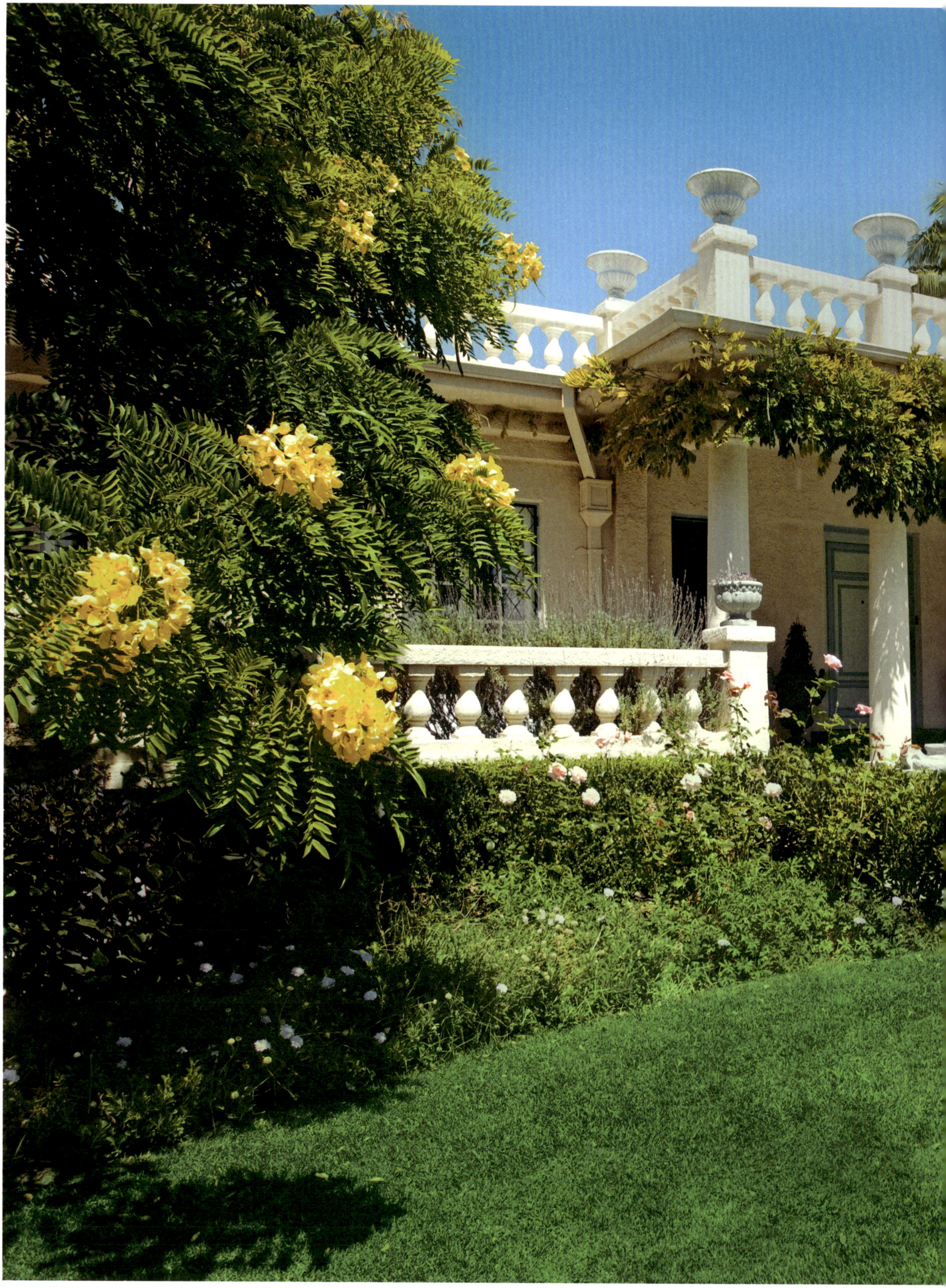

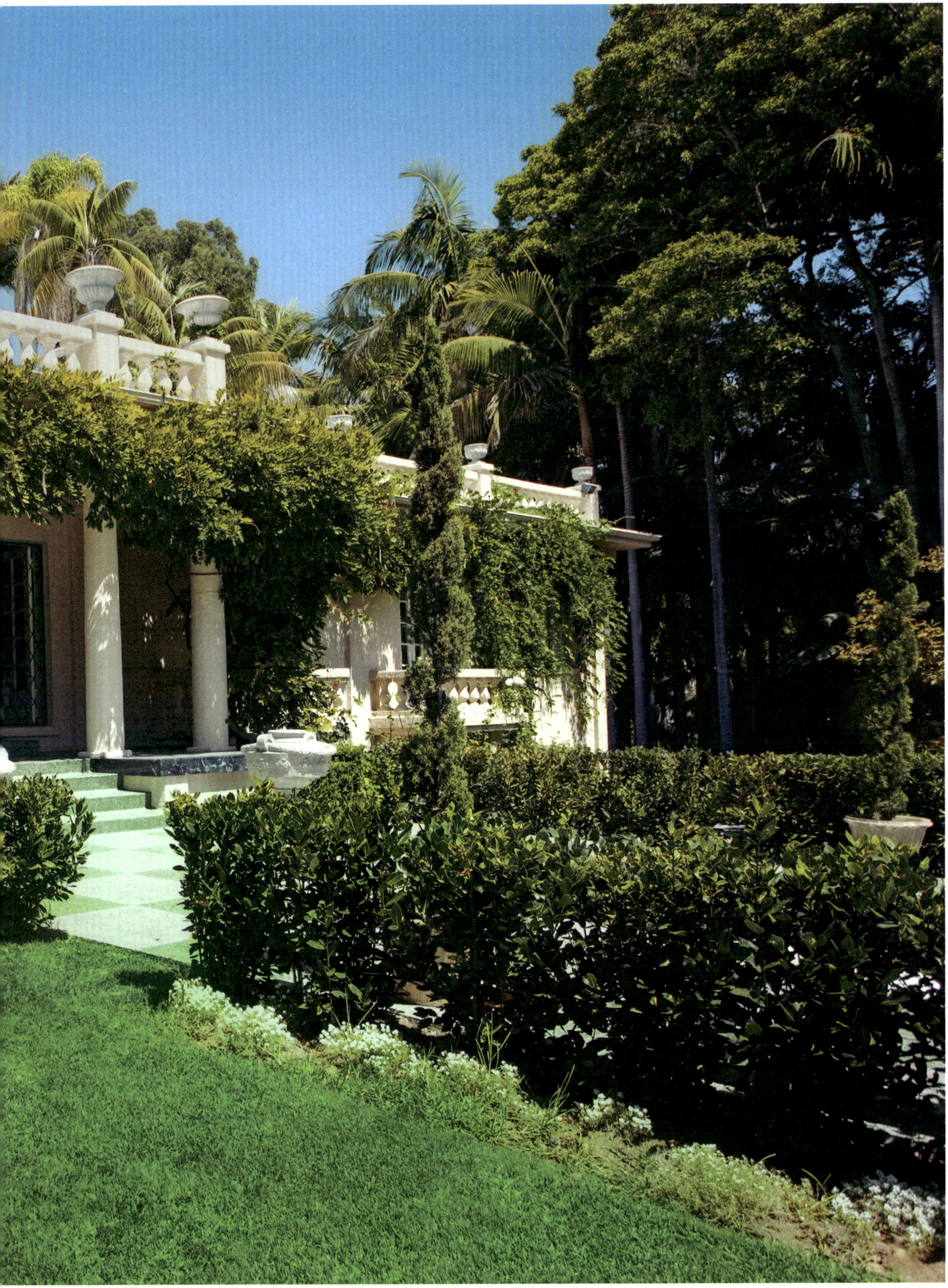

Copyright: Friends of Robinson Gardens, 2011
Publisher: Friends of Robinson Gardens

All rights reserved. No part of this publication may be reproduced, stored in a retrieval system, or transmitted, in any form or by any means, electronic, mechanical, photocopying, recording, or otherwise, without the prior permission of the Friends of Robinson Gardens.

To purchase go to: www.robinsongardens.org
The Friends of Robinson Gardens
1008 Elden Way, Beverly Hills, CA 90210

Library of Congress Cataloguing-in-Publication Data: 2011933035

ISBN 978-0-9835378-0-9

Design by Ph.D, A Design Office. www.phdla.com
Copyediting by Stephanie Emerson
The following individuals, publications, and institutions have given reproduction permission for the photographs and images produced in this book.
Robbie Anderson: p. 42 (top); Beverly Hills Public Library Historical Collection: p. 52; Glendale Public Library Special Collections: Leslie C. Brand archive: pp. 26 (bottom), 27, 28 (top); *Grand Illusions: Chicago's World's Columbian Exposition of 1893*: p. 26 (top); Barbara Bonifield Himes: pp. 14, 51; ©Timothy Lindsay: pp. 10, 64, 68, 69, 70, 71 (top left and right), 74, 76, 77, 78 (lower left and right), 79, 80, 83, 84, 86, 87, 90, 91, 96; Jeff Hyland: pp. 20, 62 (bottom); Howard D. Kelly/ Los Angeles Public Library: p. 22; Sally MacAller: p. 24 (top right); The Huntington Library, San Marino, California: p. 24 (top left); ©Tim Street-Porter: Cover (front and back), pp. 2, 4, 5, 8, 58, 78 (top left and top right), 88, 92; © Betsy Pinover Schiff: pp. 12, 13; Marc Wannamaker/Bison Archives: p. 18 (bottom); University of Southern California, on behalf of the USC Special Collections: pp. 32 (lower right), 44; Mrs. Jerry Wald: p. 56 (lower right); and Robert Woodward: pp. 30, 32 (bottom left).
All other photographs and images are from the Virginia Robinson Gardens' archives.

Printed at Blanchette Press, Vancouver, BC
First Edition
10 9 8 7 6 5 4 3 2 1

Acknowledgments

WITHOUT THE VALUABLE ASSISTANCE OF THE FOLLOWING PEOPLE AND ORGANIZATIONS, this book would not have been possible. We would like to thank Robbie Anderson; Associates of Brand Library; Carolina Barrie; Beverly Hills Public Library; David Bourassa; Blanchette Press (Kim Blanchette); Nancy Call Dowey; Echelon Color (Tony Manzella); Stephanie Emerson; Glendale Public Library, Special Collections (George Ellison); the late Ivo Hadjiev; Jesse Harris; Barbara Bonifield Himes; Jeff Hyland; Wendy Kaplan; Victoria Kastner; Ph.D, A Design Office (Michael Hodgson and Alice Joo Thomas); Tim Street-Porter and Annie Kelly; Betsy Pinover Schiff; Karun Thanni; Leslie Tillmann; The Huntington Library, San Marino, California; University of Southern California, USC Special Collections; Mrs. Jerry Wald; Marc Wannamaker/Bison Archives; Wim de Wit; Dale Witt; and Robert Woodward.

We would also like to thank our "angels" whose generous financial contributions allowed us to publish this book. They are Robbie and Jeanne Anderson, Mr. and Mrs. Martin J. Bloom, Jacqueline and Arthur Burdorf, County Supervisor Zev Yaroslavsky and the County of Los Angeles Department of Parks and Recreation, Jeff Hyland, Dorothy and Philip E. Kamins, Julia Klein, Ann Petersen and Leslie Pam, Alyce de Roulet Williamson, and anonymous donors.

Please forgive us if we have omitted someone due to oversight or press deadlines.

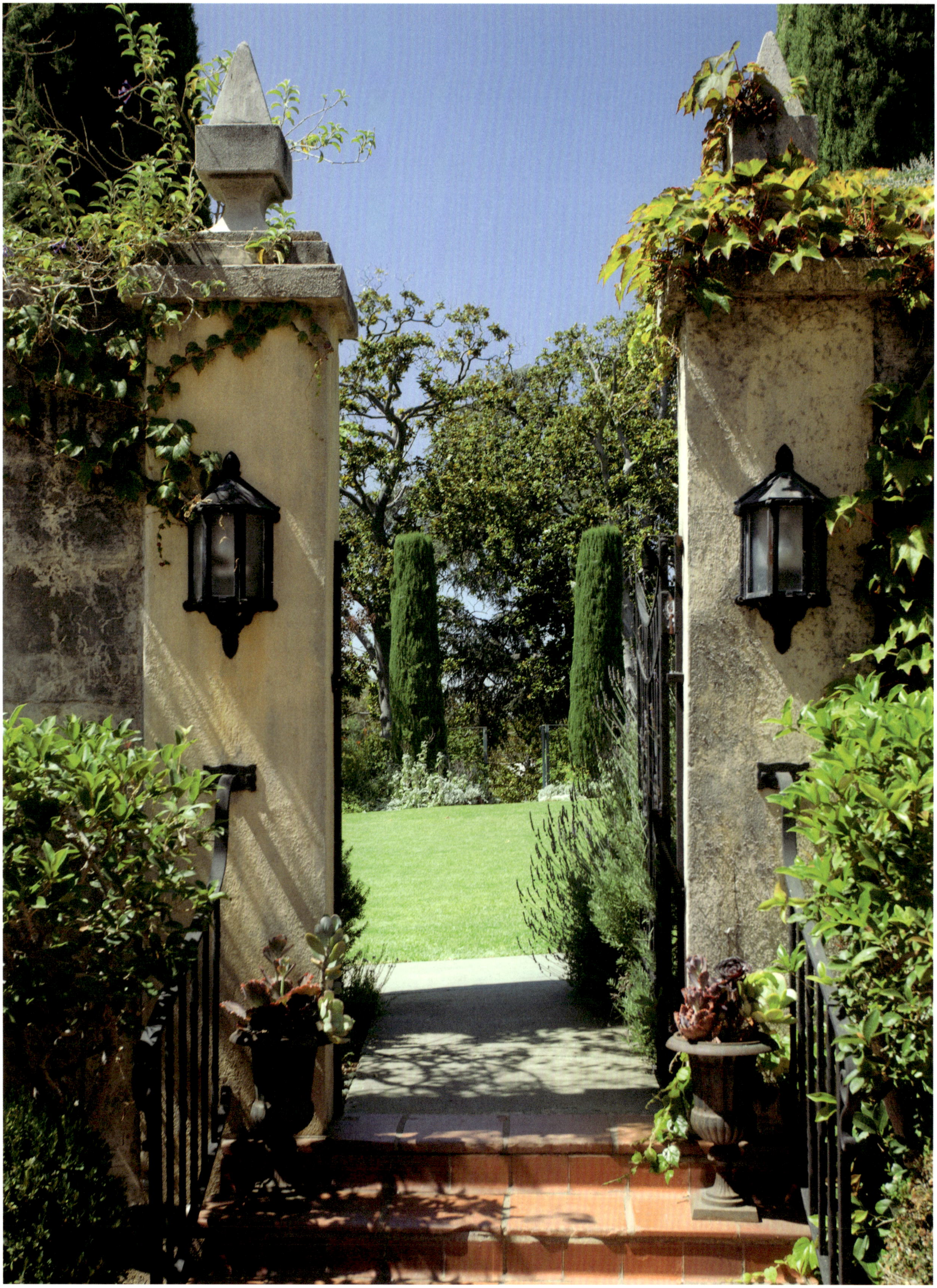

Contents

Foreword ... 11

PART I

Virginia & Harry Robinson

Introduction ... 15
Virginia and Harry's Families ... 25
    Virginia and Her Family, the Drydens ... 25
    Virginia's Greatest Influence, Uncle Leslie Brand ... 27
    Harry Winchester Robinson, His Family and the Family Business ... 29
Virginia and Harry Live the California Dream ... 33
Virginia and Harry Discover Beverly Hills ... 39
The Robinson Estate: 1008 Elden Way, Beverly Hills, California ... 43
Mr. and Mrs. Harry W. Robinson: Their Life Together ... 45
Virginia Robinson's Life as Doyenne and Businesswoman ... 53

PART II

A Walk Through the Gardens

The Gardens ... 59
The Front Garden ... 63
The Great Lawn and Dry Border ... 65
The Italian Terrace Garden ... 75
The Kitchen Terrace and The Orchid Greenhouse ... 81
The Palm Forest ... 85
The Tennis Court and The Display Rose Garden ... 89
The Virginia Robinson Gardens Today ... 93
Virginia Robinson Gardens Historical Plant List ... 94

A view to the Great Lawn from the Kitchen Terrace.

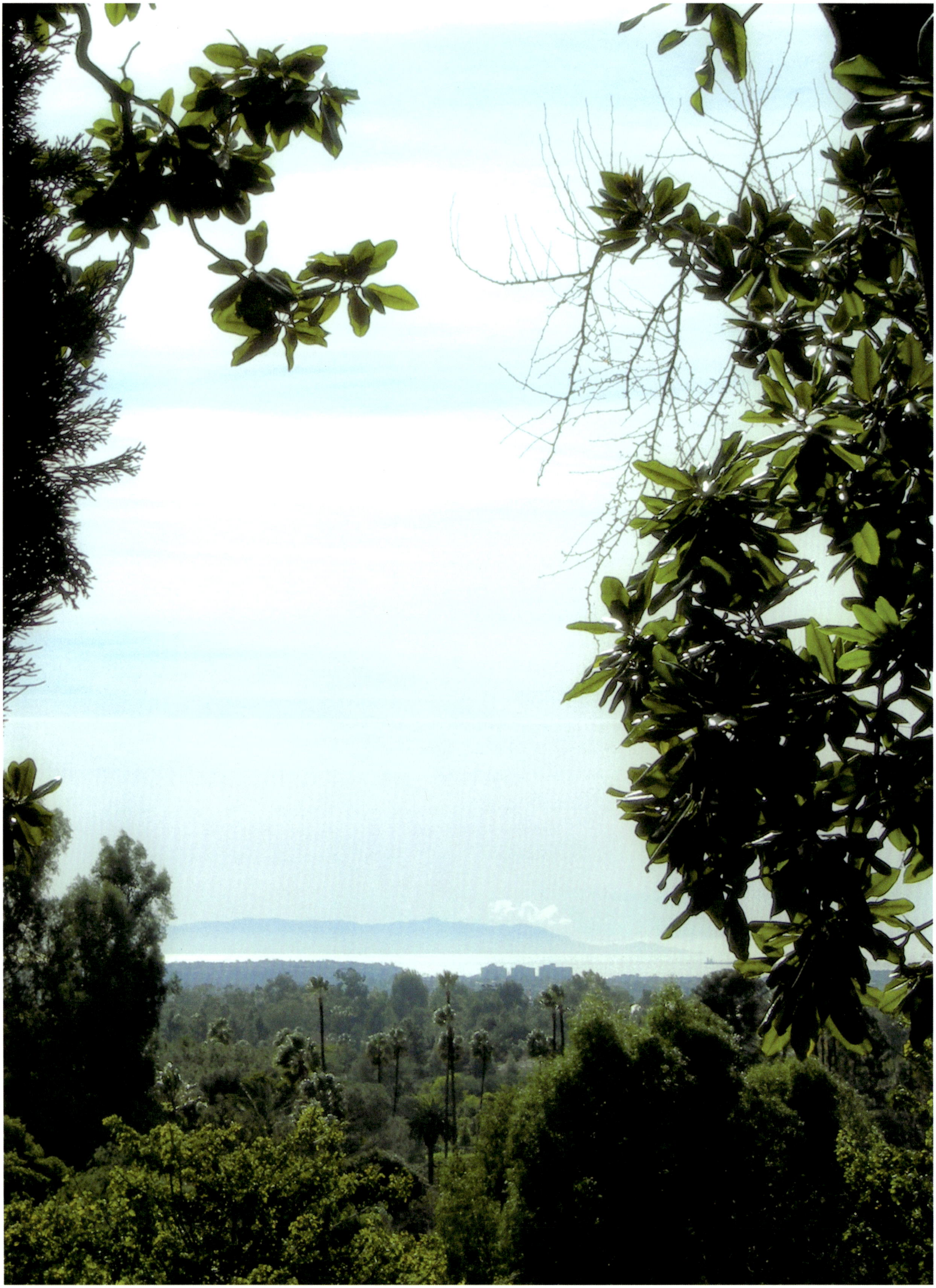

Foreword

The beautiful and glamorous city of Beverly Hills largely began on this site, at 1008 Elden Way, the home and gardens of Harry and Virginia Robinson. They were a young couple on a country drive when they fell in love with the property and purchased it on Valentine's Day 1911. At that time, this hilly landscape was almost completely empty, overlooking acres of lima bean fields below. But its views stretched out to Catalina Island. And water flowing down creeks in its nearby canyons promised the possibility of abundant gardens.

The fascinating story of the Robinsons, their house and gardens, and Virginia's longtime influence on Beverly Hills is told here for the first time. This lively and informative text will transport you back to the Beverly Hills of a century ago and bring to life one of our country's most memorable landscapes.

Victoria Kastner
Historian, Hearst Castle

Catalina Island as seen from the Italian Terrace Garden.
OVERLEAF: *The back of the Beaux-Arts style Main Residence as seen from the Pool Pavilion.*

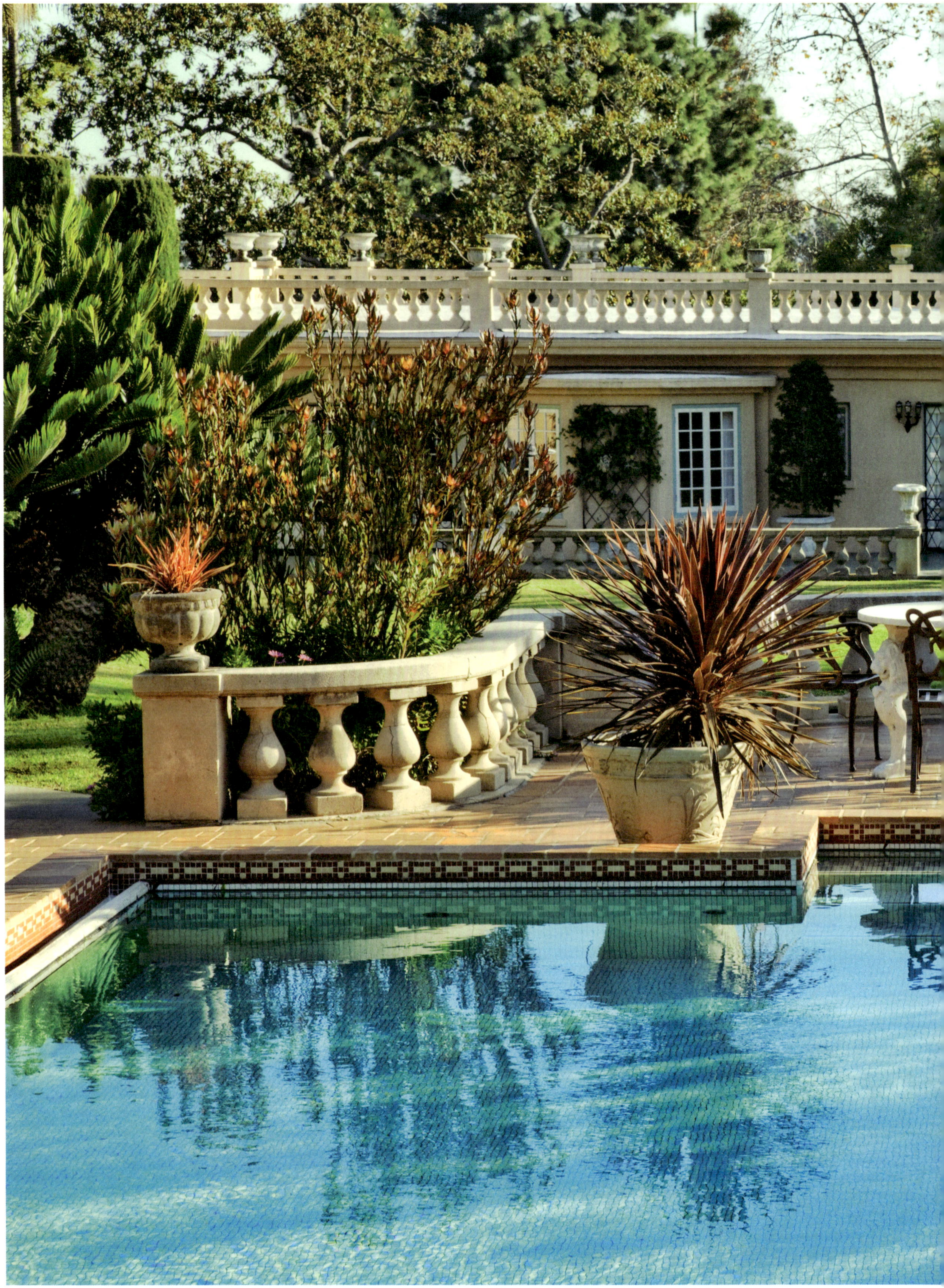

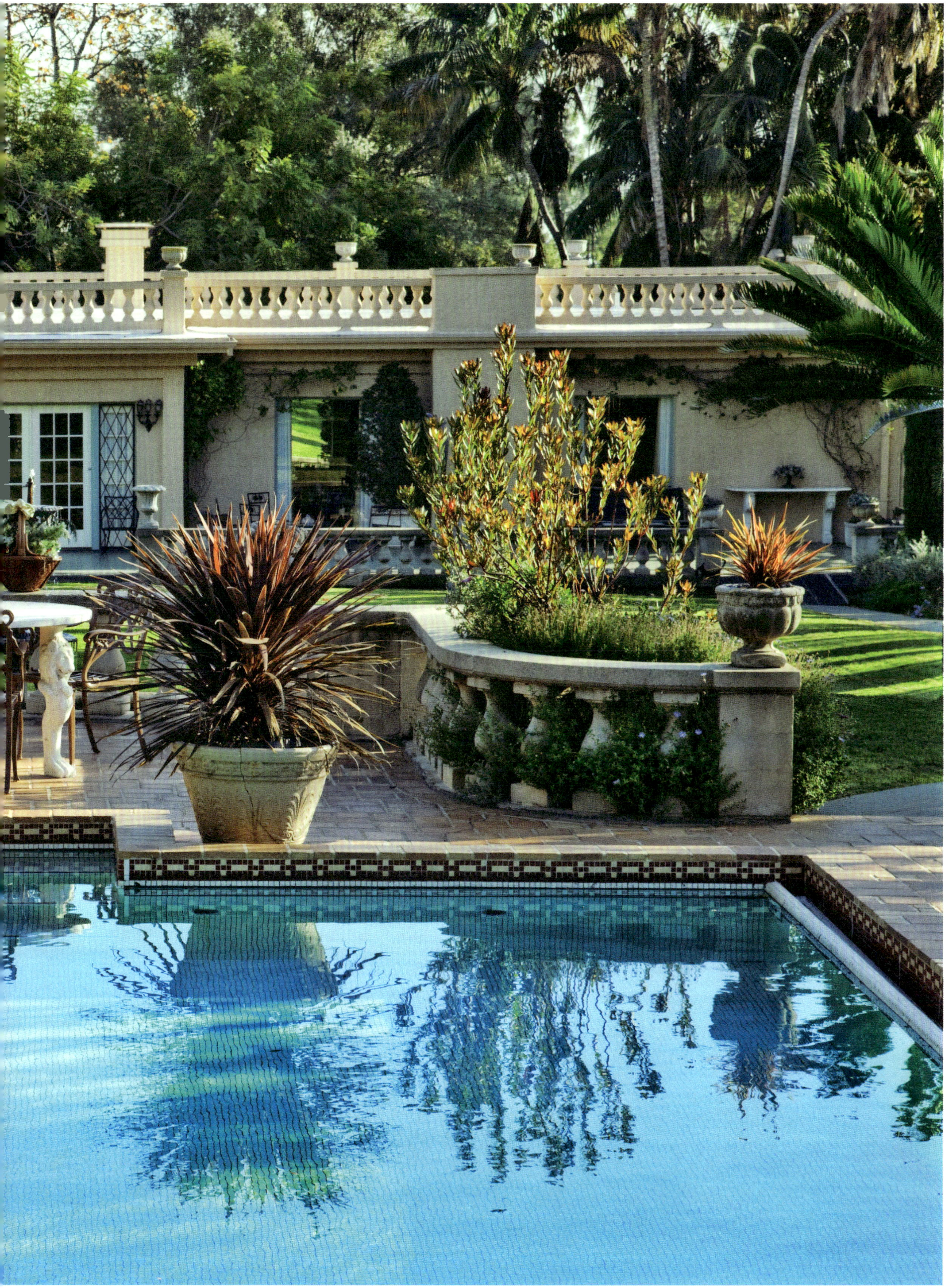

The young married couple, Virginia and Harry Robinson, stand together in a lush garden.

BEVERLY HILLS' FIRST ESTATE

PART I

Virginia & Harry Robinson

INTRODUCTION

Virginia Dryden Robinson was diminutive in stature—just slightly over five feet tall—but she made a huge impact on Beverly Hills. With her husband Harry Winchester Robinson, she helped transform this unique city into a legendary icon. Today Beverly Hills is world-renowned for its magnificent mansions, sumptuous gardens, glamorous shopping, and elusive celebrities. The Robinsons introduced this lifestyle of pleasure and privilege when they built their elegant Beaux-Arts style residence in 1911 and surrounded it with spectacular gardens. By transforming a barren hillside into a landscaped paradise, they set a standard others would follow, establishing Beverly Hills as the "Garden Capital of the World."

Like so many Californians, Harry and Virginia were originally from somewhere else. Harry was born in 1878 in Waltham, Massachusetts. The fourth generation of a family of dry-goods merchants, Harry became President of the J. W. Robinson Company, the Los Angeles department store founded by his father.

Virginia Dryden was born in St. Louis, Missouri, in 1877. The daughter of a successful builder, she was also the niece of Leslie Brand, one of Southern California's most influential entrepreneurs. Both the Dryden and the Robinson families moved to Los Angeles in the 1880s. Like countless others, they left colder regions behind, eager to come west and share in the bounties of the Southland. Both families prospered—the Drydens in construction and the Robinsons in the mercantile business. Virginia and Harry became the beneficiaries of this success and were raised in an affluent lifestyle.

Throughout their lives, Virginia and Harry continued the gracious social traditions of their youth. Family members recall weekly dinners and parties for cards, swimming, and tennis. There were many large holiday gatherings and lavish birthday celebrations. But Virginia was more than a mere socialite. She also became a successful businesswoman. Widowed early when Harry died in 1932 at age fifty-three, Virginia subsequently joined the Board of Directors of the J. W. Robinson Company and began playing an active role in its daily operations. She continued to serve on the Board through the company's most significant expansion, the building of the Beverly Hills store in the early 1950s. This location, J. W. Robinson's first suburban branch, confirmed the city's status as a high-end retail destination.

In the forty-five years after Harry's death Virginia continued to support many charities, often opening her home and gardens for worthy causes. Her diverse philanthropic interests included the Hollywood Bowl, the California Institute of Technology (also known as Caltech), the Los Angeles Music Center, and the Orphanage Guild. She was also a generous contributor to the Los Angeles County Arboretum.

Without question, Virginia's greatest act of philanthropy was the donation of her beloved house and gardens to the County of Los Angeles. When she died in 1977, just shy of her 100th birthday, she left us with a legacy that continues today. The elegant home and abundant gardens that she and Harry built together still delight visitors, year after year. The legend of Beverly Hills lives on at this estate—the first grand house and garden created in the Garden Capital of the World.

Virginia Dryden's 1903 engagement portrait. The press predicted many hearts would be broken at the news of her betrothal to Harry Robinson.

VIRGINIA & HARRY ROBINSON

{18}

Harry and Virginia's property was a barren sloping lot before construction began in 1911.

A 1920s aerial view of Beverly Hills with the foothills in the foreground. The Robinsons' estate, at the end of Elden Way, is located in the lower left.

❦ BEVERLY HILLS' FIRST ESTATE

This view of the Robinsons' estate in an early stage before the gardens matured shows the house straddling the hillside. A small gazebo in the background is adjacent to the bathing pond.

The Main Residence, the Great Lawn, swimming pool, and Pool Pavilion seen from the air in the 1980s.

BEVERLY HILLS' FIRST ESTATE

Harry's grandfather's store, H. W. Robinson & Co., was founded in the mid-nineteenth century in Brockton, Massachusetts, near Boston.

The Boston Dry Goods Store was opened in Los Angeles in 1883 by Harry's father, J. W. Robinson. It was later incorporated as the J. W. Robinson Company.

VIRGINIA & HARRY ROBINSON

The Beverly Hills J. W. Robinson department store (lower right) opened in 1952. Soon afterwards the Beverly Hilton Hotel was built next door. They occupied an ideal location near the intersection of Wilshire and Santa Monica Boulevards, the two main arteries into Beverly Hills.

BEVERLY HILLS' FIRST ESTATE

CLOCKWISE FROM TOP LEFT:

Virginia and Harry loved to entertain. They especially enjoyed dining al fresco *in the garden.*

Tennis was often a central part of Virginia and Harry's social gatherings.

Harry and Virginia hosted many lavish dinners. Tall candles illuminated this 1927 formal dinner served in their living room.

VIRGINIA & HARRY ROBINSON

{24}

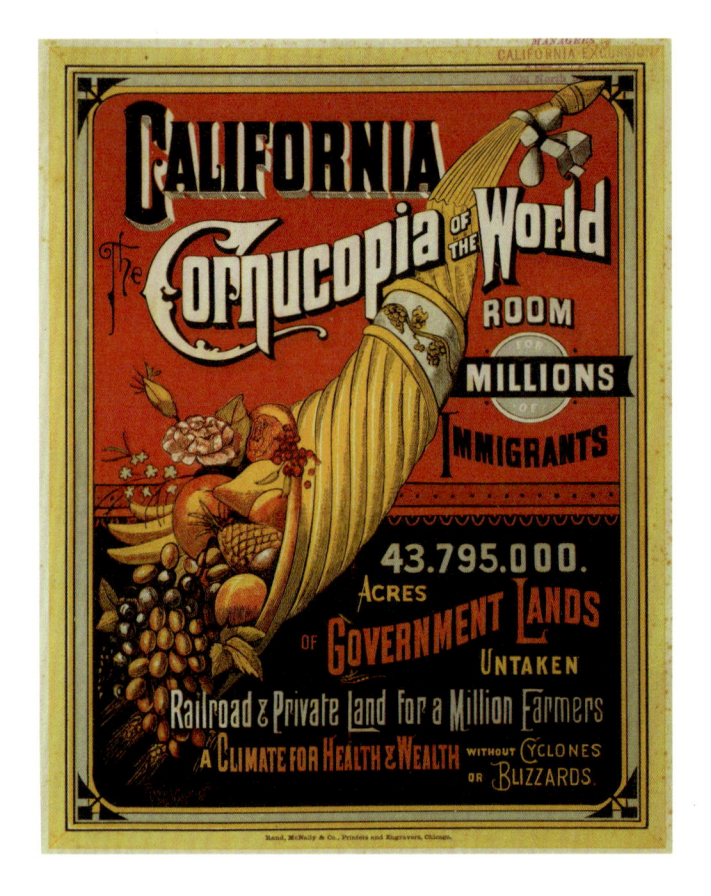

CLOCKWISE FROM TOP LEFT:

Government posters like this one publicized California's riches to the rest of the country.

The house called Ard Eevin (Gaelic for heavenly view) was built by Virginia's father Nathaniel Dryden in 1903. It was adjacent to where Virginia's uncle Leslie Brand would construct his own home a year later.

Ada and Virginia were not only siblings, they were also sorority sisters in the Gamma Chapter of the Delta Iota Chi sorority in the early 1900s.

Ada and Virginia posing together on a horse circa 1900.

❦ BEVERLY HILLS' FIRST ESTATE

VIRGINIA AND HARRY'S FAMILIES

Virginia and Harry came from remarkable families who had a profound impact on the development of greater Los Angeles. They were lured west by the promise of a better life. In the late 1880s, the "boosters"—a group of motivated locals—turned the Los Angeles Chamber of Commerce into a highly effective promotional machine. They enticed Midwesterners and Easterners with pamphlets, advertisements, and even railroad cars laden with oranges and more. With glowing language and sunny illustrations, these marketing efforts showcased Los Angeles as a cornucopia of abundance, extolling its healthful Mediterranean climate and diverse natural resources. From the mountains to the ocean, there was no limit to the good life one could achieve. Harry and Virginia's families pursued this dream and succeeded in making their fortunes. But they were dedicated to more than mere self-enrichment. Both families also helped to build the social and philanthropic institutions of this nascent city.

VIRGINIA AND HER FAMILY, THE DRYDENS

Virginia Catherine Dryden came from a tight-knit and very social family. She was born in St. Louis, Missouri, on September 21, 1877. Her father Nathaniel was a successful builder. He and his wife Helen (known as "Nellie") brought Virginia and her younger sister Ada to Los Angeles in 1887 at the urging of Helen's brother Leslie Brand. A combination of raconteur, businessman, and land speculator, Brand later became known as the "father of Glendale."

With Leslie Brand's assistance, Nathaniel Dryden became a successful architect and builder. In 1903, Brand's business partner commissioned Nathaniel to design and build "Ard Eevin" (Gaelic for beautiful or heavenly view), a West Indies plantation-style house. Even more exotic was "El Miradero" (Spanish for a high place overlooking a wide view). Nathaniel created this unique house for Leslie Brand in 1904. Both of these elaborate structures still stand in Glendale, California. Ard Eevin remains a private residence; El Miradero became the Brand Library & Art Center, commonly referred to as Brand Castle. In addition to these commissions, Dryden built more modest structures. In early 1904, he purchased a block of lots in Glendale from Brand and constructed twelve family homes. Priced from $3,500 to $4,000 each, these houses were described in the *Los Angeles Times* as having all the latest improvements.

Doubtless his most personal architectural project was the design and construction of Harry and Virginia's Beverly Hills Beaux-Arts style home in 1911. In designing their dream home, Nathaniel took full advantage of the property's sweeping vistas.

Virginia and Ada remained devoted to each other all of their lives. The siblings were sorority sisters in the Gamma Chapter of the Delta Iota Chi. Virginia was her sister's bridesmaid when Ada married William Putnam Thompson in 1902. The Drydens remained a close family after Nathaniel's death in 1924. Both sisters doted on their mother Nellie, who lived until 1937.

The East Indian Building was constructed for the Chicago 1893 World's Columbian Exposition. Its exotic architecture inspired Leslie Brand to ask his brother-in-law Nathaniel Dryden to design a home in the same style.

A silent movie, Under the Crescent, *was filmed at Brand's home, El Miradero, in 1915.*

OPPOSITE: *Virginia's uncle, Leslie Brand, was known as the "father of Glendale."*

BEVERLY HILLS' FIRST ESTATE

Although Harry and Virginia did not have children, they were very fond of Ada and William's children, Ted and Helen. They affectionately called their uncle "Robbie," a nickname based on Robinson. After Harry's death, Helen, her husband Philip Chapman, and their young daughter Ann moved in to help Virginia. Helen's granddaughter Barbara Bonifield Himes recalled that Virginia kept Helen's wedding picture on display. Virginia's nephew Ted, his wife Luigina, and their daughter Nancy Call Dowey spent a great deal of time at the estate. Nancy in particular remembers attending delightful twice-weekly parties at Aunt Gigi's, as Virginia was known. Ted was such a family favorite that Leslie Brand and Harry Robinson funded his start in business. Some years later, Ted and his wife built their home in nearby Benedict Canyon which was modeled after the Robinson and Brand estates.

VIRGINIA'S GREATEST INFLUENCE, UNCLE LESLIE BRAND

Another Dryden family member also played an important role in Southern California's growth. Nellie's brother Leslie Brand was instrumental in developing Glendale, northeast of Los Angeles. Glendale was already a thriving city when Beverly Hills was little more than a few scattered buildings and a wide expanse of lima bean and barley fields. Virginia's uncle Leslie inspired her to become a suburban pioneer in Beverly Hills.

Leslie and Nellie's family were well-to-do when he was born near St. Louis, Missouri, in 1859. Described in the press as a handsome man, Brand was five foot six, with "penetrating eyes" and a "cultivated Midwestern manner." His arrival in the Los Angeles area in 1886 was prompted by the region's first big real estate boom. When this groundswell was followed by a subsequent downturn in the market, Brand moved temporarily to Galveston, Texas, where he met and married his wife, Helen.

Before he returned to Los Angeles, Brand attended the 1893 World's Columbian Exposition in Chicago, which introduced him to a new design aesthetic. There he saw the East Indian Pavilion built in the Indo-Saracenic style. Its combination of Gothic-Revival and Indo-Islamic influences so impressed him that he asked his brother-in-law Nathaniel to build El Miradero in a similar architectural motif. Eclectic in design, it featured crenellated arches, minarets, and huge domes on its exterior and horseshoe arches throughout the interior. Its Victorian Gothic elements included ornately carved woodwork, silk damask wall coverings, and Tiffany stained-glass windows. This flamboyant house was the complete opposite of the elegantly understated Beaux-Arts style residence Nathaniel later built for his daughter and son-in-law.

Brand's April 1921 "fly-in" party included a host of Hollywood celebrities. Many flew in on their own planes. Cecil B. DeMille came in his Junkers JL-6.

Harry Winchester Robinson is shown here as a young executive in 1915.

BEVERLY HILLS' FIRST ESTATE

Brand's many successful partnerships supplied the means for his multiple houses and expensive hobbies. In 1895, he co-founded the Title Guarantee and Trust Company with attorney Edwin W. Sargent. He also partnered with the Southland's largest landowner, Henry E. Huntington. Among their enterprises was the San Fernando Mission Land Company, which in 1903 acquired a large tract of Porter's Ranch in anticipation of the 1913 completion of the Owens Valley Aqueduct. Brand also obtained the right-of-way for the electric interurban railway that ran between Glendale and Los Angeles. He later transferred his interests to a Huntington affiliate, the Pacific Electric Railway, also known as the Red Cars.

Leslie and Helen Brand's exuberant lifestyle shaped Harry and Virginia's tastes throughout their lives. Both couples embraced technology, sharing a particular fascination for automobiles. In addition, Leslie Brand owned a significant collection of airplanes and built a private airstrip on his estate. He had a retreat on Mono Lake as well as a beach house in Santa Monica. Amenities added to his Glendale property included a large two-story playhouse, tennis courts, and a pergola on its upper hillside. Brand also mingled with the Hollywood set, as did Virginia and Harry. Brand's famous 1921 fly-in party included celebrities such as director Cecil B. DeMille and silent screen actresses Mary Miles Minter and Ruth Roland.

Virginia often said that her uncle Leslie Brand was one of the most important influences in her life. He lived lavishly and entertained regularly until his death in 1925. Brand bequeathed El Miradero and eight hundred acres to the citizens of Glendale. Like her uncle, Virginia built her dream house in an undeveloped part of Southern California. At her death in 1977, she donated her beloved estate to the County of Los Angeles. Both their generous gifts ensured that the public could enjoy these historic houses and abundant gardens as an enduring reminder of Southern California's earlier days.

HARRY WINCHESTER ROBINSON, HIS FAMILY AND THE FAMILY BUSINESS

Harry Winchester Robinson came from a mercantile dynasty. The fourth generation in a family of merchants, Harry was born on October 26, 1878, in Waltham, Massachusetts. Harry was named after his grandfather, Harry Winchester (H. W.) Robinson, who expanded the family business into an emporium in the second half of the nineteenth century. Located in Brockton, Massachusetts, this well-stocked store specialized in imported carpets, tapestries, and other dry goods. Harry's parents Joseph Winchester (J. W.) Robinson and Julia Sprague Robinson also had two daughters, Alma and Louie. When Harry was four years old, the family moved to Los Angeles.

The department store Angelenos knew as J. W. Robinson and later as Robinson-May actually began as the Boston Dry Goods store in downtown Los Angeles in 1883. Upon his arrival in the Southland, J. W. opened this "carriage trade" establishment, modeled on the one that had prospered under his own father's leadership. The "Boston Dry Goods" name was meant to evoke J. W.'s New England heritage of honest and ethical trade. J. W. pledged that he would never allow

The employees of the Boston Dry Goods store awaiting a visit from President Theodore Roosevelt in 1903.

his company "to owe one cent or to be housed in a building that was not 100 percent home-owned." Store advertisements promised it would only operate on "principles of sincerity and integrity."

The exponential population growth of Los Angeles during this period contributed to the store's success. J. W.'s initial enterprise quickly outgrew its space and moved to another location on Spring Street, just opposite the courthouse. In June 1887, the *Los Angeles Times* reported that this "magnificent new store" billed as "the most extensive dry goods establishment in the city" opened with a staff of eighty employees.

The Robinson family prospered. Within a few years, they owned residences in the city and in the countryside. Their city estate, Edgemont Place, was built at the corner of Sunset and Hill Streets in 1887 by the distinguished architects Samuel and Joseph Cather Newsom. The total cost of the house and stables was the substantial sum of $10,000. Soon afterwards, the Robinsons purchased Edgemont Park, a large horse ranch ten miles outside of town in the area known today as Rosemead.

In addition to being a successful businessman and dedicated horse breeder, J. W. was also active in civic causes both local and national. An early member of the Los Angeles Chamber of Commerce boosters, he helped promote Southern California with slogans such as "California, the Cornucopia of the World," promising a "perfect climate for health and wealth." As a father of two girls, he was interested in women's education and served as a founding trustee for Miss Marsh's School for Girls, one of the earliest instructional facilities in Los Angeles. He supported worthy causes, including the National Soldiers Home in Los Angeles and the relief fund for the victims of the 1889 Johnstown Flood, a disaster that shocked the nation. When J. W. died in 1891 at only forty-five, he was honored with one of the largest funerals in Los Angeles. Harry was just thirteen at the time of his father's death.

Harry's mother Julia Sprague Robinson then became the majority shareholder of the company. She did not remain a widow for long. In the course of running the business, Julia met another merchant, C. Walter (C. W.) Randolph Ford, who with his partner J. M. (Matthew) Schneider owned a silk and tailored goods business in San Francisco. Though both men stepped in to help Julia manage the store, C. W. did more than that. He and Julia fell in love and were married in 1892. In addition to running the business, C. W. and Julia were very active in philanthropic endeavors and community projects, including her role as Patroness of the First Grand Ball of La Fiesta de Los Angeles given in 1894. C. W. died in 1896, just four years after their wedding. His obituary described how much he was liked and how he had contributed to the community. Matthew then became the President of J. W. Robinson, a position he held until his death in 1924.

Julia Sprague Robinson was a cosmopolitan woman with residences on both coasts. In 1898 she married Edward T. Barnum, a retired lawyer and investor. While on the East Coast, they lived at West 88th Street in New York City. In addition to her properties, Edgemont Park and Edgemont Place, Julia and Edward purchased an impressive Moorish-style home in Pasadena in 1902 for the

CLOCKWISE FROM TOP:

Julia and E. T. Barnum's home was located in Pasadena at 359 S. Orange Grove.

Virginia rode in the 1901 La Fiesta de las Flores parade. She is seated on the gaily decorated Chamber of Commerce float in the middle of the second row.

The Boston Dry Goods store was lavishly decorated for President Roosevelt's visit in 1903 when he headed the La Fiesta de las Flores parade in downtown Los Angeles.

BEVERLY HILLS' FIRST ESTATE

costly sum of $33,000. Located at the corner of Orange Grove Avenue and Arbor Street, the house was on a very large lot with impeccably landscaped grounds. After Barnum died in January 1905, Julia sold her city residence, Edgemont Place, to Mother Cabrini for a nominal price. A renowned social reformer, Mother Cabrini had moved from Chicago to Los Angeles to open an orphanage for children of Italian immigrants. Perhaps out of respect for her mother-in-law's memory, Virginia was a longtime contributor to a child care facility, the Maryvale Home in Los Angeles.

Julia continued to live at both her Pasadena home and her country estate at Edgemont Park until her death in 1911, that same year Harry and Virginia embarked on their world tour. Sadly, Julia died before their return. In recognition of her many contributions to commerce and charities in the Southland, the J. W. Robinson store was closed in Julia's honor on the day of her funeral.

VIRGINIA AND HARRY LIVE THE CALIFORNIA DREAM

Virginia and Harry grew up in wealth and privilege. Given the prominence of both their families, it was only natural that the two should meet, and indeed, Virginia said they knew each other as children. By the time they were teenagers, society columns listed them attending the same events.

These California youths participated in everything this burgeoning region had to offer. Both families were spirited supporters of the La Fiesta de las Flores parade, precursor to today's Tournament of Roses parade. Virginia rode on a float with a "bevy of beautiful young ladies" in the May 1901 parade and was mentioned by name in the *Los Angeles Times*, which called it the "Greatest of Crowds and Finest of Spectacles." President William McKinley headed the parade. For the 1903 La Fiesta parade, the J. W. Robinson store was grandly decorated. Matthew Schneider, then President of the company, actually knew President Theodore Roosevelt, who led the festivities that year.

During these years, Harry began his education and training to eventually become President of J. W. Robinson Company himself. After attending Throop Polytechnic Institute, now Caltech in Pasadena, he began to learn the ropes of the business. By 1900, he was an East Coast buyer for Robinson's while living with his mother and stepfather in New York. In 1901, he became a member of the Board of Directors, then departed for a buying trip throughout Egypt and India. He studied dry goods manufacturing processes and importing methods and acquired his lifelong love of travel.

By 1903, Harry and Virginia's friendship had turned into courtship. In November of that year they were married at her parents' home. He instilled in her a dedication to the family business and introduced her to the pleasures of travel.

They honeymooned on the East Coast where Harry's mother and stepfather were then located. Harry was close to his mother all of his life, as was Virginia after their marriage. All three traveled together and even shared a home together for a time. After Edward's death, they toured Europe on an extended journey, returning in November 1905. This began a lifetime of frequent

{34}

Virginia waves from the doorway of this large houseboat on which Harry and she lived while in Kashmir in 1911 during their trip around the world.

Harry invited the plantsman, Mr. Rhodes, to accompany Harry and Virginia on their 1911 trip. Mr. Rhodes assisted them in procuring exotic plants for their new home in Beverly Hills.

BEVERLY HILLS' FIRST ESTATE

trips for Harry and Virginia. Their home contains mementoes that recall some of their other sojourns. Among these are photo albums filled with pictures of their tours, a 1908 *Baedekers* guide to Egypt and the Sudan inscribed with Harry's name, and other guidebooks and travel souvenirs.

Their traveling adventures continued for the rest of their lives; their home's collections bear testimony to their journeys. Virginia and Harry's fascination with India is evidenced throughout the estate. A group of small bronzes depicting Hindu gods presides over the entry hall, a marble miniature of the Taj Mahal is displayed in the galleria, and exotic metal hanging lamps ornament the Pool Pavilion. Their love of French style can be seen in the many French porcelain figurines adorning the house. These works by Jacob Petit are decorated with the rocaille scrolls and shells emblematic of nineteenth-century rococo revival style. Virginia also loved Japan and returned there numerous times. Her library includes books on Japanese marriage and on the tea ceremony. Their far-flung destinations also included locations such as China and South America. All these varied landscapes expanded their botanical interests.

Harry and Virginia's 1911 world tour set the stage for the story of their gardens. They rode the train from Los Angeles to New York, where they boarded a steamship for Egypt. Then they visited India and rented a houseboat in Kashmir before journeying to China, Japan, and Hawaii. They brought with them the Los Angeles plantsman, Mr. Rhodes, who helped them acquire the first exotic plants for their garden. An important acquisition was the Port Jackson Fig or Walking Banyan Fig tree, which remains a distinctive feature in what would become the Palm Forest. While they were abroad, Virginia's father Nathaniel built their home.

Harry introduced Virginia to high fashion and nurtured her love for it on their many trips to Paris. A memorable occasion was their 1913 visit to the Paris salon of Paul Poiret. Considered the first modern designer, Poiret's creations featured draped lines and flowing fabrics that released women from structured tailoring and constricting corsets.

Virginia's taste and sophistication in haute couture was mirrored in the stylish clothing sold at Robinson's. She acted as a fashion plate for the store. Virginia patronized the established couture houses as well as the up-and-coming ones. Throughout the years, she often stayed at the Ritz in Paris and frequented the showrooms of many designers, including Jacques Griffe and Jacques Fath. She was both a friend and a customer of Coco Chanel. When Virginia purchased a gown from Christian Dior in December 1946, he had just opened his studio and had not yet introduced the "New Look" styles that brought him worldwide acclaim two months later.

Virginia's social and philanthropic activities kept her constantly in the press. The articles often provided detailed descriptions of her attire. The *Los Angeles Times* columnist Brandy Brent placed Virginia on the Southland's Best Dressed Women's list for 1950 and described her thus: "Ageless, youthful in heart and figure, she takes her beauty swathed in [Gilbert] Adrians and [Hattie] Carnegies to the best drawing rooms of the nation." Along with Mrs. Louis B. Mayer and

{36}

JACQUES GRIFFE
SOCIÉTÉ ANONYME
AU CAPITAL DE 100.000 FRANCS
10, RUE DES MOULINS, PARIS-1er
TÉL. : 742 57-53
R. C. PARIS 69 B 2704

N° 1

Very charming dress of
printed polka dots chiffon
red & black   4.700 frs

BEVERLY HILLS' FIRST ESTATE

Virginia (on left) chats with her dear friend Perle Mesta, who was U. S. ambassador to Luxembourg from 1949–1953. Virginia is wearing a diamond necklace, earrings, and brooch.

A 1913 receipt from the important French fashion designer Paul Poiret for one of the purchases Harry and Virginia made while visiting his salon in Paris.

OPPOSITE: *Virginia's personal files include this Jacques Griffe dress design with fabric samples.*

VIRGINIA & HARRY ROBINSON

{38}

CLOCKWISE FROM TOP:

Virginia and Harry loved to go fishing on their boat, the Cornell.

Virginia poses next to her Duesenberg automobile used in the 1934 movie, The Gay Divorcee, *with Fred Astaire and Ginger Rogers.*

Harry and Virginia adventurously drove their stout little Franklin automobile through the snow over the Sierras.

BEVERLY HILLS' FIRST ESTATE

Gloria Swanson, Virginia was named one of the twelve chicest women in Southern California.

Virginia also had a passion for jewelry and fine furs. Some of her jewels had impressive pedigrees, including a twenty-five carat diamond brooch formerly part of a nineteenth-century British tiara and a ruby brooch once owned by Napoleon. Other stunning pieces were an eighty-carat diamond necklace and a thirty-carat tremblant diamond pin. Although she left much of her estate intact, Virginia bequeathed her collections of clothes, jewelry, and furs to family and friends. Among the fortunate recipients was Dolly Green, daughter of Burton Green, one of the developers of Beverly Hills, whose estate was nearby.

In addition to luxury objects, Virginia and Harry enjoyed games, sports, and physical activity. They lived socially active lives that often included playing bridge and dancing. They were energetic tennis players, adventurous boaters, and avid anglers. Though Harry caught a few, it was Virginia who won many trophies and ribbons, including the prize in 1908 for reeling in a large yellowtail. The following April, Virginia caught a white sea bass weighing forty-four pounds while fishing off Seal Rock. The next year, she won the Tuna and Tackle Club's Burns Cup pennant—also for the largest yellowtail, weighing forty-three pounds. A close call at sea came in 1908. With distress signals flying because their boat was half-full of water, the Robinsons had to be rescued off San Clemente Island. Even this near disaster did not end their love of boating or fishing.

The couple embraced advancements in transportation technology and was among the first to buy automobiles. Today it is difficult to imagine getting a mention in the newspaper for purchasing a car. But in April 1906, the *Los Angeles Times* announced that a Columbia Stanhope-Victoria had just arrived for Mrs. Harry W. Robinson of Pasadena. Shortly after, Harry's acquisition of a new Franklin was similarly heralded. The paper also chronicled their successful drive to the summit of the Sierras in July 1907 in an article headlined: "O'er Snows in Motor Car. Sierras' Top is reached by daring motorist. Runabout races over deep drifts in safety. Light car tows heavy auto on devil's slide." The photo album documenting this achievement was proudly displayed in their home for many years. They subsequently owned three Duesenbergs, still considered one of the best automobiles ever built. This coveted car gave rise to the expression: "It's a Doozy!" Ginger Rogers drove one of the Robinsons' Duesenbergs in the 1934 film *The Gay Divorcee* with Fred Astaire.

VIRGINIA AND HARRY DISCOVER BEVERLY HILLS

Harry and Virginia echoed their parents' pioneering spirit when they decided to build on a barren hilltop in the budding subdivision called Beverly Hills. The area at that time had a long history of unsuccessful development.

In early 1822, María Rita Valdez and her husband Vicente Ferrer Villa settled on a 4,539-acre ranch called *Rodeo de las Aguas,* or "gathering of the waters." This name refers to the streams of

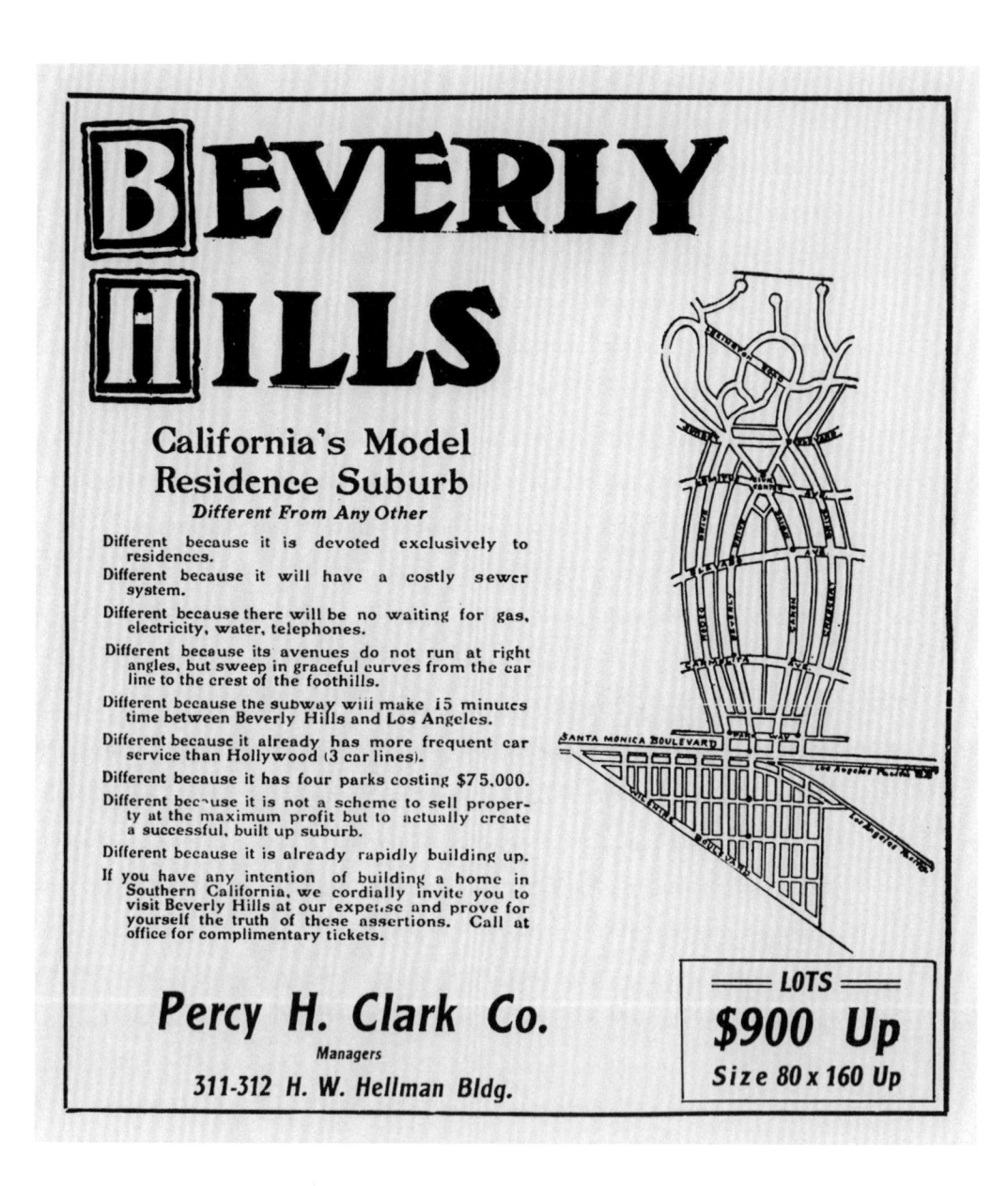

BEVERLY HILLS

California's Model Residence Suburb

Different From Any Other

Different because it is devoted exclusively to residences.

Different because it will have a costly sewer system.

Different because there will be no waiting for gas, electricity, water, telephones.

Different because its avenues do not run at right angles, but sweep in graceful curves from the car line to the crest of the foothills.

Different because the subway will make 15 minutes time between Beverly Hills and Los Angeles.

Different because it already has more frequent car service than Hollywood (3 car lines).

Different because it has four parks costing $75,000.

Different because it is not a scheme to sell property at the maximum profit but to actually create a successful, built up suburb.

Different because it is already rapidly building up.

If you have any intention of building a home in Southern California, we cordially invite you to visit Beverly Hills at our expense and prove for yourself the truth of these assertions. Call at office for complimentary tickets.

Percy H. Clark Co.
Managers
311-312 H. W. Hellman Bldg.

LOTS $900 Up
Size 80 x 160 Up

A variety of advertisements for the Beverly Hills suburb appeared regularly in the Los Angeles Times.

water rushing down from the canyons in the rainy season, creating swamps or *cienegas*. In 1831, this tract (officially known as "San Antonio") was granted to María Rita and her relative, Luciano Valdez. Due to conflicts between them, she purchased Luciano's interest in August 1844 for $17.50. The property was later sold to Major Henry Hancock and Don Benito Wilson. They and subsequent owners failed at farming. With the discovery of oil in Los Angeles, the Pioneer Oil Company purchased the drilling rights. Unable to make a big strike, Pioneer subdivided and sold off the parcels.

In the 1880s, Charles Denker and Henry Hammel purchased most of this land to raise crops to feed the guests at their United States Hotel in Los Angeles. After Edward Laurence Doheny struck oil near the La Brea Tar Pits in 1905, "black gold" fever once again took hold. In 1906, the venture group Amalgamated Oil Company purchased a large tract of the Hammel and Denker Ranch. Instead of oil, they struck water. Thereafter a group of oilmen and land developers—including Henry E. Huntington, Burton E. Green, W. S. Porter, Charles A. Canfield, and W. G. Kerckhoff—founded the Rodeo Land and Water Company. Their goal was to develop the suburban real estate project they named Beverly Hills.

Conceived as a subdivision for the wealthy, Beverly Hills offered amenities such as water, sewer, gas, and streetlights. Its curving streets were paved and featured sidewalks and curbs. Planted along these were rows of trees identical in size. Each street featured a different type of tree, including oaks, elms, and pepper trees. Typical of the many optimistic advertisements extolling the subdivision's popularity was an ad in the November 1906 *Los Angeles Times* claiming that sales in Beverly Hills were doubling—with "Millions Behind It [and] Millions Before It, Beverly Hills is indeed a paradise—a wonderland." This onslaught of promotion emphasized the "intelligent conception" of the new development. The ads frequently invoked the name of Henry Huntington, one of the wealthiest men in the country. His role as an investor was evidence that this project was of the "finest quality."

The Rodeo Land and Water Company made the inspired choice of hiring Wilbur David Cook, Jr. and engaged him to design a master plan for this upscale community. One of the nation's foremost landscape architects and community planners, Cook was a perfect match for the assignment. While working for Frederick Law Olmsted—arguably America's greatest landscape architect—Cook helped design the 1893 World's Columbian Exposition in Chicago. He also participated in redesigning the grounds of the White House in 1902 and created city parks for both Boston and Chicago. By 1905, he had left Olmsted's Massachusetts firm and headed west to lay out a system of parks for Oakland, California. After accepting the Beverly Hills commission, Cook moved to Los Angeles, where he also planned Exposition Park, the lower slopes of Griffith Park, and the grounds of the Los Angeles Civic Center.

Cook proposed a brilliant three-tiered plan for Beverly Hills. He had the foresight to understand that without a place for the daily services, help-staff, and shops, a subdivision for

The Los Angeles Country Club opened in 1911 at its present location near Beverly Hills. Virginia and Harry were driving to the club when they made a wrong turn and found the property on which they built their dream home.

The Robinson estate at 1008 Elden Way photographed shortly after its completion in 1911.

BEVERLY HILLS' FIRST ESTATE

wealthy homeowners would not succeed. The first tier was for commercial use, located below a traditional urban boundary—the railroad tracks on Santa Monica Boulevard. The middle tier extending up to Sunset Boulevard consisted of residences for affluent families. The third tier rose above Sunset, providing larger lots for the elegant houses and estates, whose size and status increased with the elevation.

THE ROBINSON ESTATE: 1008 ELDEN WAY, BEVERLY HILLS, CALIFORNIA

They were on a drive to the new site of the Los Angeles Country Club when Harry and Virginia stopped at a location just above Sunset Boulevard. Virginia later said that they took a wrong turn on their way to the Club and found themselves at a lovely knoll. The property offered magnificent views to Catalina Island, some twenty miles out into the ocean. To the east were the snow-capped peaks of the San Bernardino Mountains. They immediately decided to build their home on this dramatic site. Virginia and Harry bought the property within forty-eight hours and signed the closing papers on Valentine's Day of 1911. This was one year before the Beverly Hills Hotel was built and three years before Beverly Hills officially became a city. As the hillside's earliest residents, Harry and Virginia demonstrated their keen judgment and eye for beauty.

Virginia's father Nathaniel Dryden designed and built the home while Harry and Virginia travelled around the world. The official account provided in *The Los Angeles Builder and Contractor* in February 1911 described the project:

> Nat Dryden, 1555 Manhattan Place, has prepared plans for a large concrete residence to be erected at Beverly Hills for Harry W. Robinson, 2068 Hobart Boulevard, proprietor of the Boston Store. It will be a one-story structure, 133 x 96 feet, designed in the Italian style of architecture. The construction will be entirely of reinforced concrete. There will be twelve rooms, with white cedar and white enamel finish, oak floors, plate glass windows, five marble mantels, four tile bathrooms, furnace, plumbing and electric fixtures. The estimated cost is $25,000. The construction will be done under the supervision of Mr. Dryden, who will also let all sub contracts.

The house was located near the crest of the property, oriented to provide spectacular views of the mountains, the ocean, and distant landscapes of the fields below. Its siting also allowed for nearby vistas of what would become the magnificent gardens. This building straddled the knoll, creating space for a lower level at both ends. On the west end, a barren hollow later became the Italian Terrace Garden. It was initially planted with citrus, olives, and pomegranates. The view from the front door down Elden Way revealed Baldwin Hills in the distance and many undeveloped lots below Sunset Boulevard. Virginia's dressing room afforded blissful views to the azure blue sea all the way out to Catalina Island. Even today, although the vista is partially obstructed

In 1914, the J. W. Robinson store relocated to a larger building on Seventh Street in downtown Los Angeles.

by several structures, in the afternoon a soft breeze still blows in from the Pacific, providing natural air conditioning throughout the entire house.

The Robinsons' home provided a dramatic setting, perfect for entertaining indoors and out. Its spacious public rooms all feature ample seating areas. Many of these spaces open to the surrounding gardens. The loggia on the east side of the house had no exterior wall or roof separating it from the outdoors. This design concept epitomized the California way of life where the interior space merges into the landscape.

Harry and Virginia began their long residency in their new house on September 30, 1911. On the front leaf of her guest book, Virginia wrote this date along with her touching comment: "The first night in our home." Over many ensuing months, she recorded details of the parties she and Harry hosted, including menu plans and guest lists.

One of the estate's most impressive features is the Pool Pavilion which was modeled after the Villa Pisani estate in Stra, Italy. This Palladian structure was initially built in 1925. It included a solarium, two guest rooms, and two kitchenettes. In early 1929, it was enlarged to include a billiard room and the upstairs card room. It exemplifies the Beverly Hills lifestyle—informal activities amidst formal buildings. The Pavilion's imposing presence is softened by the inviting turquoise-blue water of the swimming pool. Although the house (or "Main Residence") sits atop a knoll, the Pool Pavilion is on a significantly higher grade, giving it prominence in the landscape. Virginia and Harry were most likely inspired to create the Pavilion in homage to the playhouse her Uncle Leslie constructed behind his house. The swimming pool and the Pavilion became a focal point of many pleasurable activities for Harry, Virginia, and their guests.

Throughout the years of their residency, the Robinsons added onto and altered various elements of their estate. They remodeled and expanded the galleria and partially enclosed the loggia. Harry and Virginia added the Staff Quarters and a men's tennis court as well. They also built more garages as their fleet of cars grew. But in all its essential aspects, the estate's charming layout remains much the same today.

MR. AND MRS. HARRY W. ROBINSON: THEIR LIFE TOGETHER

Harry and Virginia were prominent figures in the Los Angeles business community and became the cornerstone of Beverly Hills culture. In the early years of their marriage, Harry began his climb up the career ladder at Robinson's. Upon his return to Los Angeles from Egypt and India in late 1902, he became involved in the company's day-to-day management. By 1909, the *Los Angeles Times* referred to him as proprietor of the Boston Dry Goods store. Not long after, Harry supervised its 1911 expansion. Business grew so much that in 1914 the store moved to a larger location on Seventh Street between Grand Avenue and Hope Street in downtown Los Angeles. In 1924, Harry Robinson became President of the company. At nearly six feet tall with handsome

CLOCKWISE FROM TOP LEFT:

The Hollywood director George Cukor (on left) was a close friend and neighbor of Virginia's.

For larger parties, Virginia placed dining tables throughout the house, including in the entrance hall.

Buff Chandler, the philanthropist and Los Angeles Times *heiress, was Virginia's close friend and frequent guest at her bridge parties.*

Agnes Moorehead and Buddy Rogers chat by the pool at a party.

BEVERLY HILLS' FIRST ESTATE

features, Harry's geniality made him one of the most popular department store executives in Southern California. He also was an active member of the most important clubs in Los Angeles: the California Club, the Los Angeles Country Club, and the Crags Country Club.

The Robinsons used their estate as a venue to entertain their friends and business associates as well as to host charity events. Over the years they gave magnificent parties, including the annual Patroness kick-off party for the Hollywood Bowl and the annual August Moon party held on the evening of the full moon. It truly was a gathering place, and among their neighbors were many celebrities. Loretta Young and her husband Tom Lewis, Mary Pickford with her first husband Douglas Fairbanks, Jr. and later her second husband Buddy Rogers, director George Cukor, Ethel Barrymore, and Irene Dunne were just a few of the renowned guests who enjoyed the Robinson's hospitality.

The newspapers were replete with society column articles about the fabulous parties at the Robinsons. Mrs. Violette Nason, a woman also considered to be a leading social doyenne of her time, went to some of the most important events in Los Angeles and Beverly Hills during her long life of 101 years. She said many times that the most exciting event she ever attended was a party at Mrs. Robinson's home.

Virginia and Harry entertained using every part of the estate depending on the occasion. On special nights, the antique entry hall carpet was rolled up to provide a dance floor. The dining tables might be set up in the entry hall or living room, as well as in the dining room. Events were also hosted in the Pool Pavilion and other locations throughout the gardens. Douglas Fairbanks, Jr.'s hunting lodge (later known as Pickfair) was just up the hill, and he and his close friend Charlie Chaplin joined in the Robinsons' festivities. Fairbanks' athletic stunts and Chaplin's hilarious antics must have enlivened these occasions. Fred Astaire played tennis on the Robinsons' courts as gracefully as he danced on film.

A helicopter landing was one of the most unusual events to take place at the estate. Walt Disney's widow Lillian invited Virginia to Florida for the grand opening of Disney World in 1971. Her helicopter touched down on the Great Lawn behind the Main Residence and whisked Virginia off to John Wayne Airport for their flight to Orlando.

Many of Harry and Virginia's guests were captured on paper thanks to the skill of the talented actor and artist Roland Young. A dear friend of the family, he was godfather to Nancy Dowey, Virginia's grandniece. Though most famous for his acting—in particular his title roles in the *Topper* films—Young was also a gifted illustrator. He published *Not For Children*, a clever volume of his caricatures and poems. He also drew many lighthearted portraits of Harry, Virginia, and their guests. Particularly touching is a sketch of Harry dressed for tennis. This one-of-a-kind scrapbook exists at the estate today, providing not only an historical record but also an incomparable glimpse into Harry and Virginia's lives.

CLOCKWISE FROM TOP LEFT:

Harry (left) and tennis pals goof around on the court.

Harry (right) and a friend frolic in the pool while riding their whimsical animal-shaped floats.

The artist Roland Young caricatures a swimmer diving over one of the animal floats.

Roland Young captures Harry, both in profile and in mid-swing, while playing tennis.

BEVERLY HILLS' FIRST ESTATE

The last head of the staff, majordomo Ivo Hadjiev, gave an overview of how Virginia planned her parties. He recalled they usually began with "the lady" choosing her designer dress. Then flowers for the party arrangements were picked from the garden—their colors chosen to match her outfit. To signal the close of the evening, the staff served chamomile tea to the guests. Finally the many candles were snuffed out, one by one. When Virginia was once asked why everyone always had such a good time at her parties, she said, "If the hostess has a good time, so will everyone else." She always did.

Harry and Virginia not only loved their family and friends, but they also adored their pets. They were particularly devoted to their dogs, both mixed-breed and pedigreed. Their photo albums show numerous pictures of them playing with their dogs. Virginia's affection for dogs extended to her serving as the patroness for the first all-breed dog show of the Kennel Club of Beverly Hills.

Pets were not limited to dogs, but included resident monkeys, flocks of parakeets, cockatoos, and other exotic birds. George, the desert tortoise who lived in the Dry Border of the Great Lawn, would on occasion crawl through the French doors to sleep beneath Virginia's bed. Barbara Bonifield Himes, Virginia's great great-niece, remembers as a child feeding the little bunnies who ventured out from under the cypresses. Harry saw their first monkey, a capuchin, in a downtown pet store window and felt so sorry for him that he bought the monkey and brought him home. In all, three generations of monkeys lived at the estate. They roamed the property freely until the terrified neighbors complained. Afterwards they resided in their own very large monkey cage. Many of these beloved pets were buried on the property and given their own head stones. Barbara Himes said her family's longstanding tradition has been "loving animals as family members and discipline is never truly enforced!"

A fatal stomach ailment ended Harry's life on September 19, 1932. He would have turned fifty-four the following month. His funeral was held at their home with close friends and family members in attendance. The same minister who had married Harry and Virginia—Reverend Hugh K. Walker—conducted the service. Harry W. Robinson was buried at Forest Lawn Memorial Park in Glendale. As had been done for his mother and father, the J. W. Robinson Company was closed on the day of his funeral to honor his memory.

Upon Harry's death W. L. Valentine, Harry's brother-in-law and member of the Board of Directors, became President of J. W. Robinson. He briefly served in that capacity until J. Walter Schneider, the son of a previous Robinson president, was elected to the position in May 1934. Virginia joined the Board at this time and commenced her leadership role in the company as her mother-in-law Julia had done when Harry's father died.

Harry loved to play with his pets.

Curious guests watch with bemusement while Virginia shows off her mischievous monkey.

Virginia enjoys a moment with George the desert tortoise. Family friend Carolina Barrie recalled that George occasionally came into the house and would spend the night underneath Virginia's bed.

J. W. Robinson's elegant Beverly Hills store shared the corner lot with Conrad Hilton's chic Beverly Hilton Hotel.

Virginia (left) wore her suite of magnificent moonstone jewelry—a necklace and large earrings—as part of her costume at one of her fancy-dress parties.

BEVERLY HILLS' FIRST ESTATE

VIRGINIA ROBINSON'S LIFE AS DOYENNE AND BUSINESSWOMAN

Virginia lived another forty-five years and never remarried. She continued to travel and still hosted both formal and casual events. Late in life, she reminisced, "I lead the same life today that I always have, though I miss Harry."

She was a modern woman, active not only in society and charities but also in business matters at J. W. Robinson. In late 1938, her attorney detailed the corporate strategies Virginia made or advocated. She was instrumental in merchandising decisions such as the change in the buyers for sportswear, women's corsets, and menswear. She improved the store's fabric selection to complement the creation of a dressmaking department. She wisely advocated for the expansion of the parking lot to accommodate the ever-growing number of automobiles. In addition to overseeing the building's exterior and interior improvements, she remodeled the employee cafeteria and tried to convince the Board to open a public restaurant inside the store. After these achievements, she stepped back and hired a day-to-day operations executive who reported directly to her. Nonetheless, as a member of the Board, Virginia continued to attend all Directors' meetings.

In anticipation of building a new store in Beverly Hills in 1947, J. W. Robinson purchased Gilbert Adrian's atelier in Beverly Hills. Adrian was a favorite Hollywood designer, best known for dressing Greta Garbo, Jean Harlow, and Joan Crawford. He designed custom couture for his stars and had created costumes for over 250 movies. The company intended Adrian's chic address to serve only as its temporary location until its substantially larger complex could be built.

J. W. Robinson's beautiful and spacious Beverly Hills store opened in 1952 near the corner of Santa Monica and Wilshire Boulevards, east of the Los Angeles Country Club. Conrad Hilton's Beverly Hilton Hotel occupied the adjacent parcel. Both companies agreed to share the 1100-car parking lot. As befitted this key location, J. W. Robinson lavished six million dollars on the building's construction. Designed by the famed modernist architects William Pereira and Charles Luckman, this store was built with the finest materials; its exterior was finished in Vermont marble and Brazilian granite. Among the architects' other Southland projects were the Theme Building at the Los Angeles Airport and the Disneyland Hotel. Renowned industrial designer Raymond Loewy conceived the store's elegant interior. The prolific and talented landscape architects Florence Yoch and Lucile Council created its landscaping plan. J. W. Robinson's arrival solidified Beverly Hills' status as a destination for high-end shopping. Thousands attended its first-day festivities, which were copiously profiled in the *Los Angeles Times*.

Although Virginia's active involvement in the company ended in 1955 when Associated Dry Goods Corporation bought the family business, she maintained her schedule of parties, get-togethers, and philanthropy. She generously opened her home and garden for many good causes. Among the largest gatherings she hosted at her estate was the annual Hollywood Bowl Patroness Benefit, referred to in the press as the hottest ticket in town. The kickoff to the Bowl's summer

CLOCKWISE FROM TOP LEFT:

Virginia (fourth from left with butler standing behind) hosts a dinner in the Pool Pavilion in 1934.

Virginia (second from right) and guests pose in the entrance hall at one of her many costume parties.

Virginia wears some of her fabulous jewelry at a pre-dinner toast for The Bachelors, a philanthropic men's organization.

BEVERLY HILLS' FIRST ESTATE

season, this party for four hundred started promptly at six o'clock. All the guests departed equally promptly at nine o'clock. Virginia orchestrated her events in the same spirit as she lived her life—with precision and pleasure.

An invaluable window into her days comes from majordomo Ivo Hadjiev's oral history. A native of Sofia, Bulgaria, he worked for Virginia during the last decade of her life. Subsequently he became the curator of the estate and remained there until his death in 2008. While Virginia's friends knew her as a relaxed and approachable person who loved to get out in the garden in her rubber boots, she expected her staff to be properly attired in their uniforms. Each staff member was assigned to a specific duty. In addition to maintaining the services of two accountants and two lawyers, Virginia had a household staff of twelve. This included a personal secretary, four butlers, a chauffeur, a Cordon-Bleu trained chef, a sous chef, and a kitchen maid. Ivo said twelve gardeners maintained the six-and-a-half-acre estate. He proudly recalled, "We had the biggest staff in all of Beverly Hills."

Ivo continued the impeccable standards developed by his two predecessors over a half a century. He recalled with pride that he never took a seat in Mrs. Robinson's presence, even when Virginia offered him one. Every morning he stood behind her as she worked on her correspondence and invitations at her desk. At each meal, he also remained behind her chair, ready to assist. On Monday mornings, he helped her prepare three weekly menus: "One for the lady, one for the staff, and one for the parties."

In 1975, *Town and Country* magazine named Ivo Hadjiev one of the sixteen heads of staff recognized nationwide with the honorary title "Master Majordomo." Ivo asserted that this award was not merely for his dedicated service, but rather for the highly refined lifestyle Mrs. Robinson had established. Her loyal staff made Virginia and Harry's home a success and the Robinsons generously shared its benefits with countless guests.

Virginia maintained her mental sharpness, vitality, and *joie de vivre* all her life. A swimmer into her eighties, she spoke of going for a swim the morning after her New Year's Eve party in order to get out the kinks from dancing a new step the night before. She was a popular dance partner and insisted on dancing as a feature of her parties. She took walks nearly every day, epitomizing the healthy California lifestyle. She also loved the excitement and mental stimulation of card-playing, especially bridge. She played frequently with many of her guests, including Charles Boyer, Agnes Moorehead, and Buff Chandler. Buff's family owned the *Los Angeles Times*, and like Virginia, she was a civic benefactor. She raised the funds to build the Music Center in Los Angeles, and she served as a University of California Regent. Buff and Virginia were close friends who shared a lifelong dedication to improving the social and cultural resources in their communities.

CLOCKWISE FROM LEFT:

Virginia and her majordomo Ivo Hadjiev look out at the Pacific Ocean from the Santa Monica cliffs.

Virginia poses with the director Vincente Minnelli in her entry hall.

Major Polan with Virginia at a concert. Both he and Virginia shared a passion for camellias.

BEVERLY HILLS' FIRST ESTATE

Virginia died on August 5, 1977, just forty-four days short of her one-hundredth birthday. Emulating her uncle, Leslie Brand, Virginia Robinson donated her estate for the public to enjoy. It was her life's accomplishment and the place she loved more than any other. Today the estate is owned and maintained by the County of Los Angeles with assistance from the Friends of Robinson Gardens, a support group which raises funds for the estate's preservation. The buildings and grounds flourish under the expert attention of Timothy Lindsay, Superintendent of the Virginia Robinson Gardens.

Harry and Virginia took a barren hill atop Elden Way and created their own image of paradise. In so doing, they brought to life the vision of the founders of Beverly Hills. This elegant estate inspired others to pursue building their own dream homes nearby. The luxury trade fostered by the J. W. Robinson store bolstered the city's growing reputation as one of America's greatest shopping districts. Virginia and Harry's glamorous parties substantiated this city's world-wide reputation as a location where celebrities meet and mingle. Virginia Robinson truly deserves her designation as the First Lady of Beverly Hills. When asked once how long it had taken to complete her home and gardens, she responded, "A lifetime." And thanks to her generosity, all of us can enjoy what she and Harry built––for many lifetimes to come.

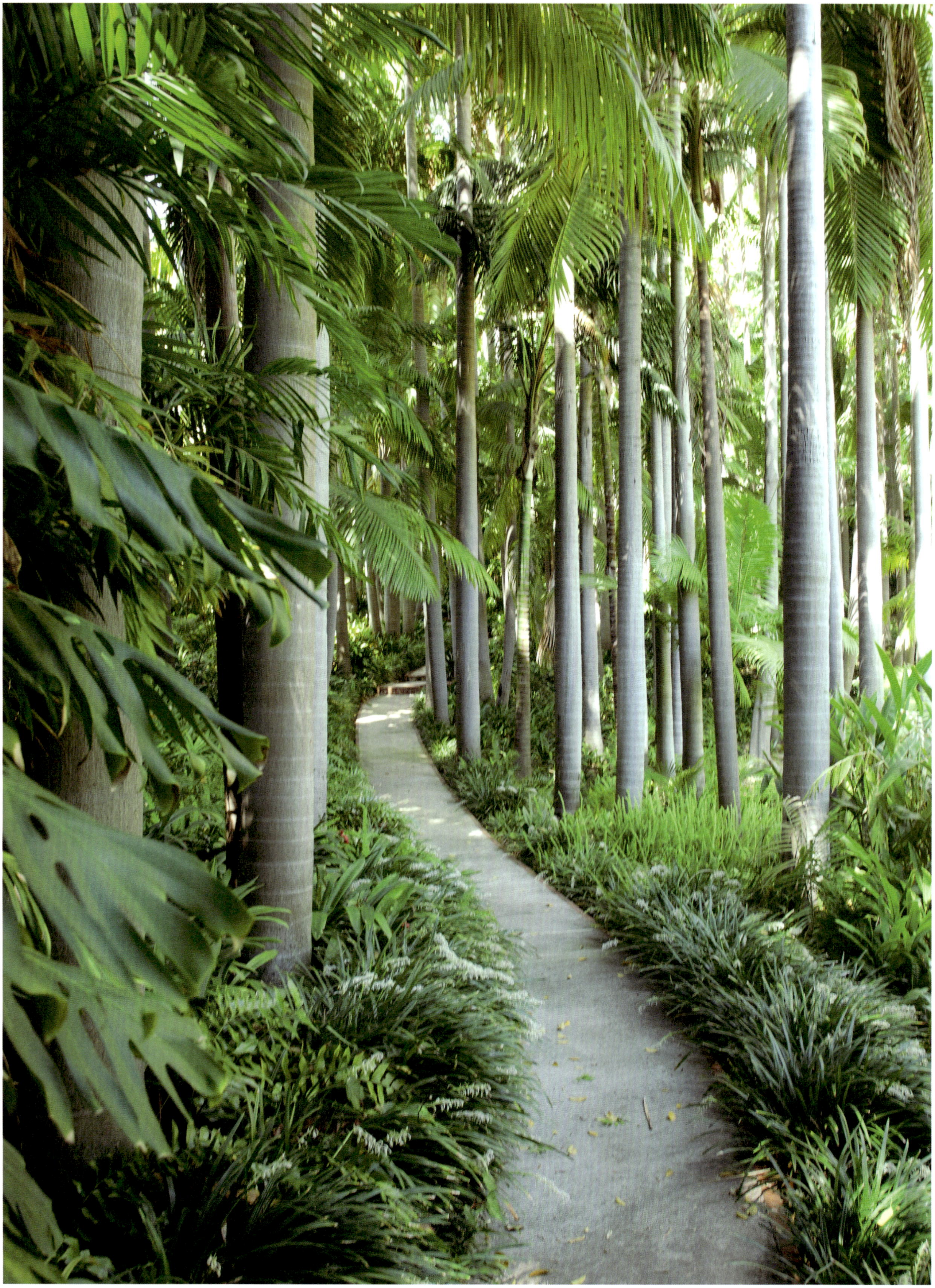

PART II

A Walk Through the Gardens

THE GARDENS

The planning and planting of their "villa garden," as Virginia affectionately referred to it, began in 1911, immediately after Harry and Virginia moved into their new residence. The cultivation of gardens, a passion for them both, was vital because the house sat on a hill surrounded by bare earth that had been overgrazed by cattle and sheep during the Mexican rancho period. Virginia said, "There was just one lonely tree growing on the property when we bought it; I think it was called a Blue Elderberry tree."

The Santa Monica Mountains, the general geological locale of 1008 Elden Way, had been coaxed up from the sea bottom over a period of eons by a succession of earthquakes. The result was a soil that was fertile and well-drained. While the Main Residence of the estate is at 480 feet above sea level, to the east and west there are hollows that create microclimates, which provide prime habitat for exotic gardens.

A footpath meanders through several acres of Australian King Palms, the largest known collection outside of Australia.

Most plant introductions flourished in this Mediterranean climate, defined by long, hot, dry summers followed by a rainy season that spans November through April. The average annual rainfall of sixteen inches was supplemented by irrigation with ground water and imported water from the High Sierra Mountain range in central California. Most Easterners thought the gentle climate "benign" compared to the extreme weather they had left behind them. The Pacific Ocean lies only seven miles to the west of the property. The Alaskan current hugs the coast, and its average temperature of sixty-two degrees Fahrenheit buffers the gardens from extreme heat and cold and allows more plants species to be grown here than anywhere else in the continental United States.

During the next sixty-six years, five distinct gardens were created at Elden Way. For protection from the elements, gardens were first established near the house, starting with the Front Garden. As time, ideas, and money allowed, gardens were developed further away from the house. These individual gardens were developed gradually and methodically and now command their place among the great American estate gardens of the early twentieth century.

Harry and Virginia often started plants from seeds or cuttings that came to them from around the world, provided by friends or nurserymen. They also gained inspiration by visiting faraway gardens while on their travels. Consequently, the gardens host a plant palette that can be traced back to nearly every continent. In Alma Whitaker's interview, "Mrs. Harry Robinson Known Widely as Perfect Hostess," published in the *Los Angeles Examiner*, January 21, 1934, Virginia stated, "I am almost a professional gardener." She was noted for her experimental plantings of rare trees, including the area's first successful mangos and many new varieties of avocados.

Both of the Robinsons loved to watch things grow and loved to share their gardens with family and friends. As the gardens matured, they became the main venue for entertaining. The Great Lawn, the primary location for large parties, was used to accommodate up to 400 guests for sit-down dinners with an orchestra and a dance floor in the middle of the lawn. During the warmer months the solitude and ambiance of smaller gardens, such as the Palm Terrace, offered space for the Robinsons and their guests to play bridge or read.

Six to twelve gardeners tended the garden depending on the season and the year. The head gardener for many years was Lino Benedetti, who oversaw the entire six-and-half-acre estate. Early on plants had to be hand watered using hose-pipes and hose-end sprinklers.

In addition to the Robinsons, many hands were involved in the development of the gardens. When planning the Palm Forest, for instance, the couple consulted with landscape architect and President of the City Planning Association of Los Angeles, Charles Gibbs Adams, who worked for many prominent movie people, including director Cecil B. DeMille, a friend of Virginia's Uncle Leslie Brand.

Bill Evans was a plantsman who worked principally for Walt and Lillian Disney, helping Walt source and develop the properties for his amusement parks. He also consulted on the Disney's Carolwood Drive residence in nearby Holmby Hills. Since Virginia played bridge with Lillian Disney, she was often able to convince her friend to let Evans consult at the Robinson estate as well, an arrangement that continued for several decades. Bill Evans made his last visit to the Robinson estate in the summer of 1998, twenty-one years after Virginia's passing. He complimented the plantings in the Dry Border and the many other restoration efforts in the garden. He said that the level of refinement he observed would have truly pleased Virginia.

Julius and Don Nuccio, of Nuccio Nursery in Altadena, recommended many of the azaleas and camellias in the garden and developed a close relationship with Virginia. At the suggestion of Virginia's dear friend Major Polan, Nuccio's developed a camellia named "Virginia Robinson" in 1957. This camellia grows twelve to fourteen feet tall and is covered with pink semi-double flowers. Virginia named one of her white camellias Coco Chanel after her friend, the designer, and often wore a real camellia rather than the silk versions that came with her Chanel dresses.

To see which trees would grow the best, the Robinsons experimented by planting a variety in the Front Garden. Virginia is surveying the young trees from the front porch.

The view to the southeast from the front porch of the Main Residence shortly after the Robinsons moved into their new home. Lima beans and barley are growing in the fields in the distance.

BEVERLY HILLS' FIRST ESTATE

THE FRONT GARDEN

An early photograph of the estate's Front Garden shows a lawn and a dozen or so small trees planted in a random pattern. Presumably this was a trial to see which trees might survive and provide shade to the house, which was exposed to all the elements, especially the relentless afternoon sun of August and September. The view from the front door looking down Elden Way was mostly lima bean fields, without a single structure or tree in sight. The concrete walkway ran straight from the street to the front door. During the 1950s, a more formal entry was added, including a terrazzo plaza with a central planter where a statue of Cupid was placed. At that same time, the driveway and pedestrian gates were built along the street with a four-foot stucco wall to provide privacy and visual interest.

Many of the original plantings remain in the Front Garden. The Tulip Magnolia was planted where Virginia could admire it while sitting in the morning room where she sorted through her mail and planned her menus. When in bloom, the white-and-purple wisteria vines over the front porch created Virginia's favorite spot to be photographed. The Bay Laurel hedge growing on each side of the driveway is original to the Robinsons' plantings, and this type is used in other areas when restoring hedges on the property. There are several citrus trees, a scenic grove of Kentia Palms, and two Himalayan laurels still growing on the south slope of the Front Garden. As one approaches the estate from Elden Way, two Southern Magnolias stand stately and tall guarding the pedestrian gate. These eighty-year-old trees, the oldest in the Front Garden, originally provided shade for the gate man as he waited to assist the arriving guests.

In 1974, Virginia and the five members of the County Board of Supervisors planted a yellow flowering tree outside the library, the Golden Medallion tree (seen on front cover of book), in recognition of the donation of her property to the County of Los Angeles.

The walkway originally ran straight to the front door from the street. Virginia is standing in the doorway of the house which is covered by creeping fig.

A WALK THROUGH THE GARDENS

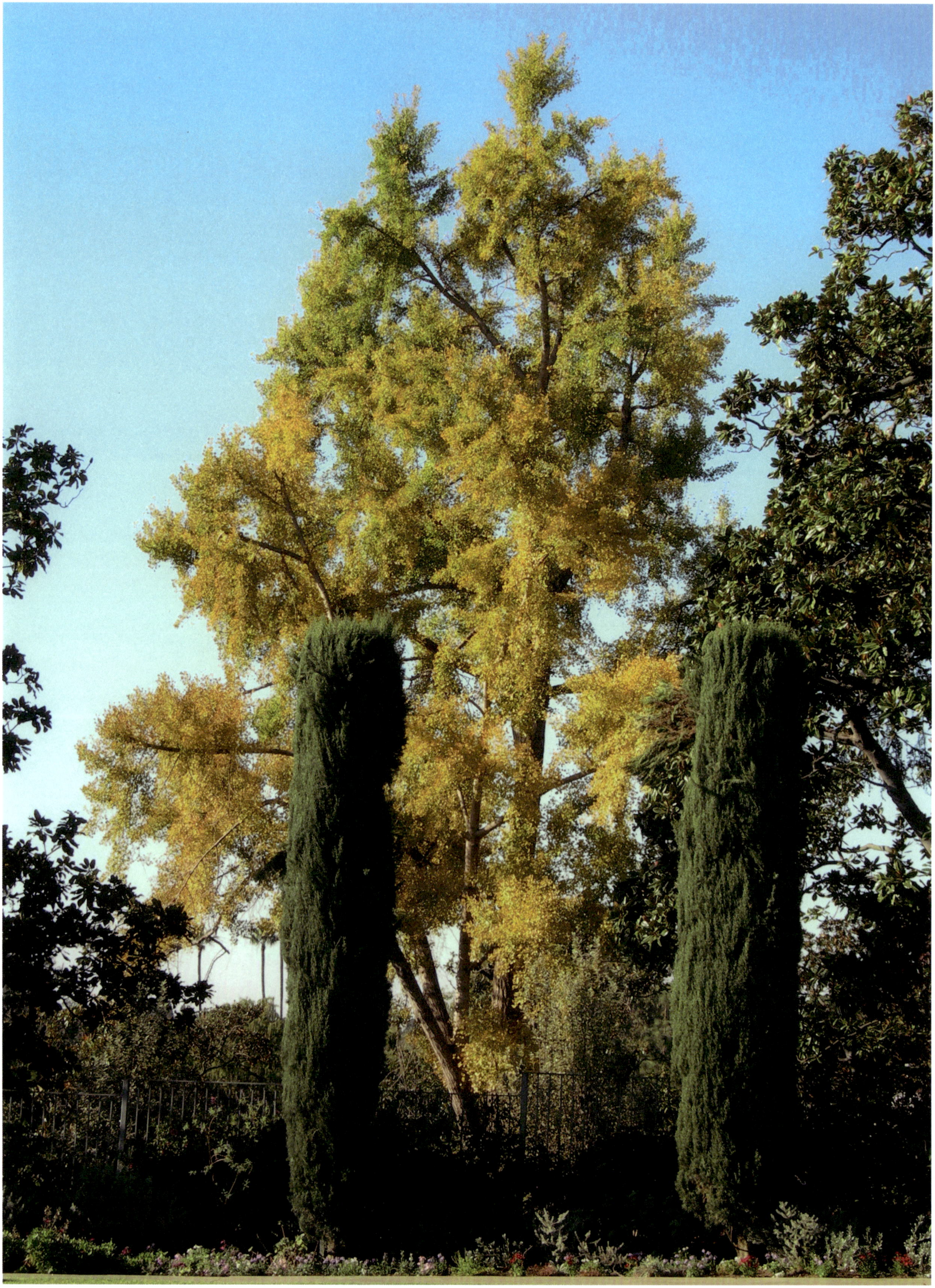

THE GREAT LAWN AND DRY BORDER

The 10,000-square-foot Great Lawn is planted in a native South African grass called Kikuyu. This lawn serves as the carpet to what could be considered an outdoor room, enclosed by the Residence and the garden walls. Early on, there was a bathing pool positioned on the rise at the northwest end of the lawn; located below this were two rectangular lily ponds. A gazebo covered with vines was built next to the bathing pond. On occasional hot summer nights, dry ice was added to the bathing pond so the vapors would cool those reclining under the gazebo.

In 1925, when the Pool Pavilion was built, the two lily ponds in the lawn were removed, and the bathing pond was partially filled in and converted to a lily pond. The pool deck was constructed to create an alcove above the pond and a marble table from Pompeii, Italy, was placed there for small luncheons. The gazebo was removed and standard oleanders were planted to create shade and interest when they flowered.

When the large swimming pool was installed, it had a secondary function: to enhance the architecture of the Pool Pavilion by reflecting its details on the smooth, mirror-like surface of the water. The pool's blue color and one-inch square tiles with a Grecian key mosaic pattern drew many visitors to compare the pool to the one at Hearst Castle, located in central California.

In order to visually connect the Residence and Pool Pavilion, eighteen columnar cypress trees, nine planted up each side, flank the Great Lawn. Each tree is pruned two inches shorter than the previous one as they move up the slope towards the Pool Pavilion, resulting in the last cypress being sixteen inches shorter than the first (a practice still maintained today). This technique creates the illusion of a greater elongated space between the Main Residence and the Pool Pavilion. The forced perspective draws the viewer's attention to the exquisite Italian Renaissance architecture of the Pool Pavilion, which sits at a higher elevation than the Main Residence. For this reason, the swimming pool in front of the Pavilion is not visible from the Residence. As one walks towards the Pavilion, the pool appears as a wonderful surprise.

A Dry Border is planted between the cypress trees on each side of the Great Lawn. The perennials in this area are from the Mediterranean regions and have similar water requirements to the cypress. The Dry Border brings color, texture, and seasonal interest to the space. Growing in the northwest corner of the Border is the Red Powder Puff tree, which blooms continuously with scarlet flowers. It became one of Virginia's favorites, and she always paused as she passed by it on her afternoon walks in the garden. In her later years, she walked the garden twice a day, once in the morning and again after lunch, accompanied by Ivo Hadjiev, her last majordomo, who made notes of her directives for the gardeners. Hadjiev would routinely scout the garden prior to her walk to make sure that no hoses had been left out in the sun when not in use. This was one of her pet peeves and would certainly land the gardeners in trouble.

The yellow Ginkgo was one of Virginia's favorite trees for autumn color.

{66}

❦ BEVERLY HILLS' FIRST ESTATE

A friend stands in the shade of the gazebo while watching Virginia and the others enjoy the bathing pond.

OPPOSITE ABOVE: *The gazebo was located at the northwest end of the Great Lawn as seen from the Main Residence.*

OPPOSITE BELOW: *Virginia is walking on paving stones next to the newly planted Cypress trees which flank the Great Lawn.*

OVERLEAF: *A Dry Border was planted between the columnar Cypress trees, which provide a dramatic perimeter to the Great Lawn. A rainbow can be seen in the sky.*

A WALK THROUGH THE GARDENS

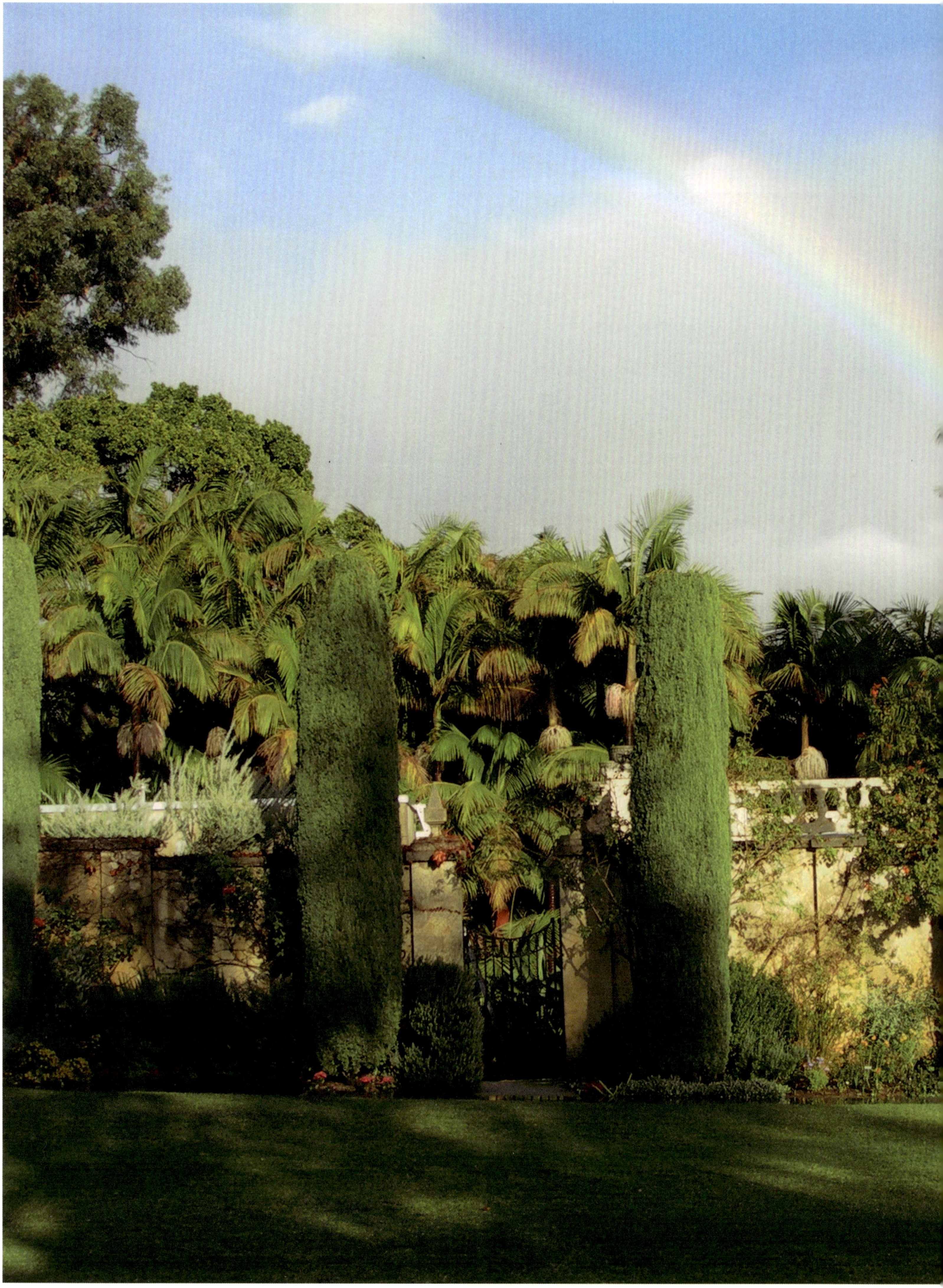

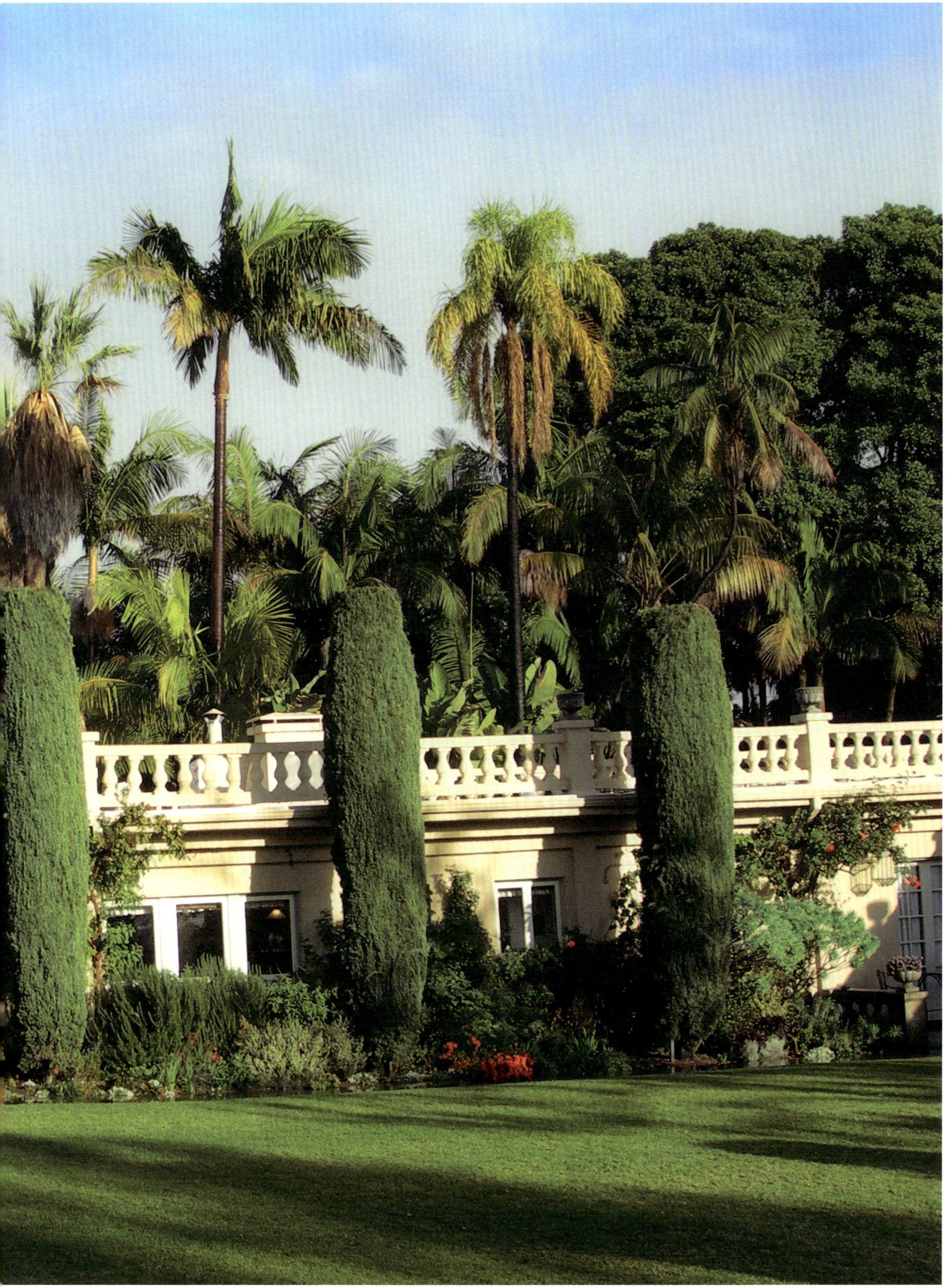

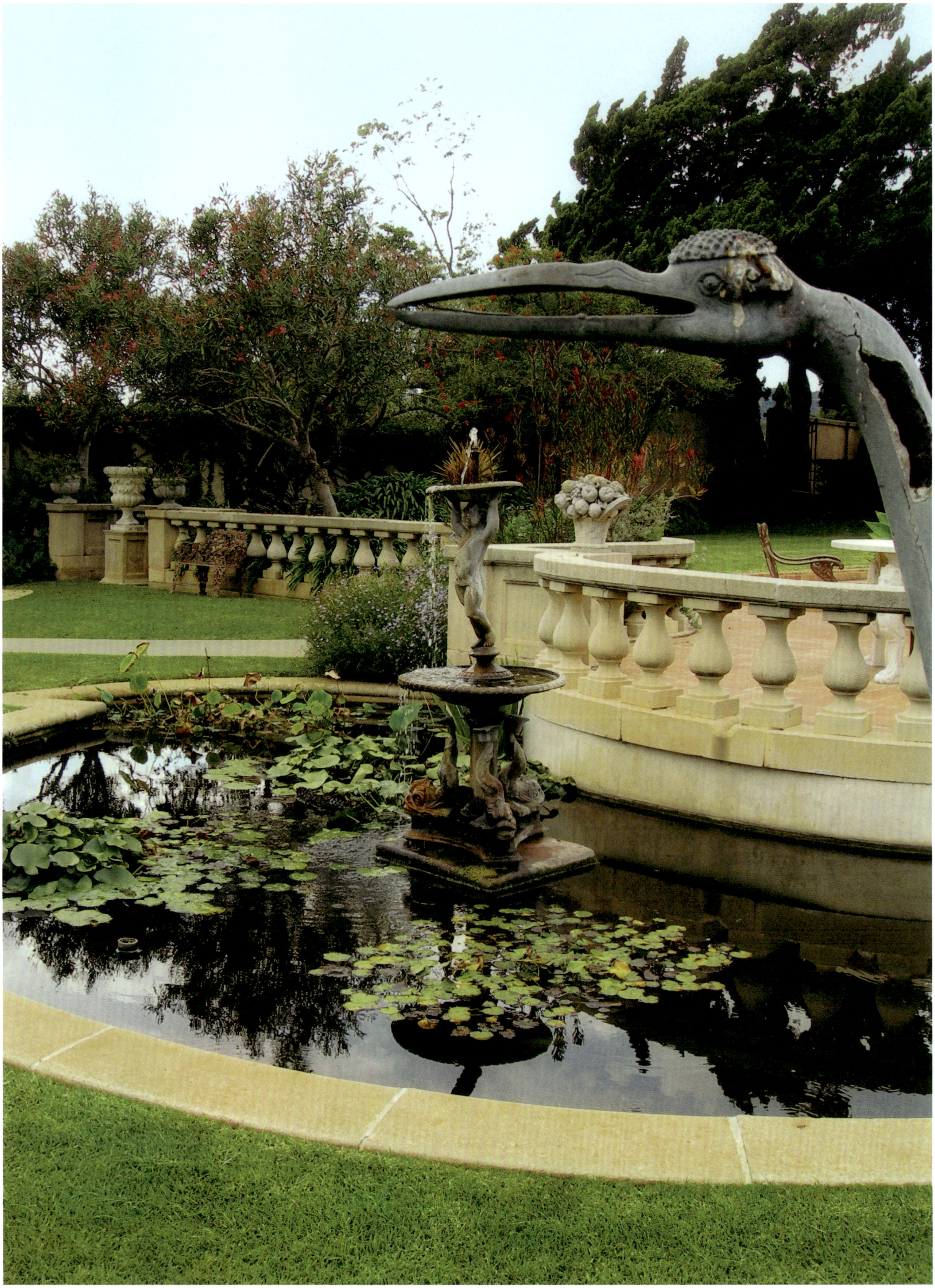

CLOCKWISE FROM TOP LEFT:

The Citrus Terrace is planted with limes, lemons, and tangerines.

The Red Powder Puff tree, which blooms profusely nearly year-round, grows in the Dry Border.

The surface of the swimming pool serves as a mirror reflecting the Roman arches of the Pool Pavilion.

OPPOSITE: *The bathing pond was converted into a lily pond after the swimming pool was built in 1925.*

OVERLEAF: *Inspired by the Villa Pisani in Italy, the Pool Pavilion is the architectural jewel of the estate. The Robinsons referred to it as "the playhouse." Inside it offers a billiard and card room while outside there is a swimming pool and tennis court.*

A WALK THROUGH THE GARDENS

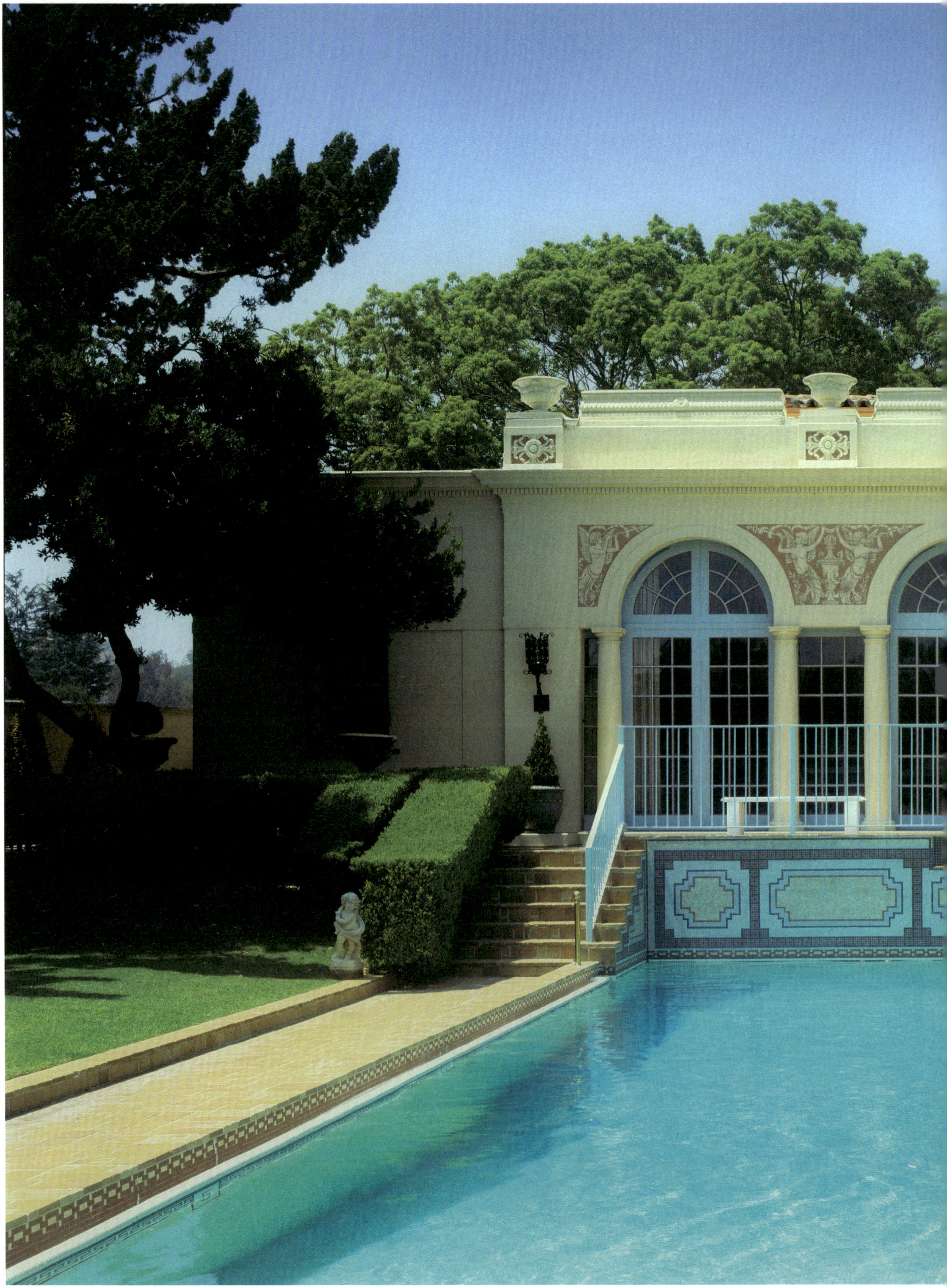

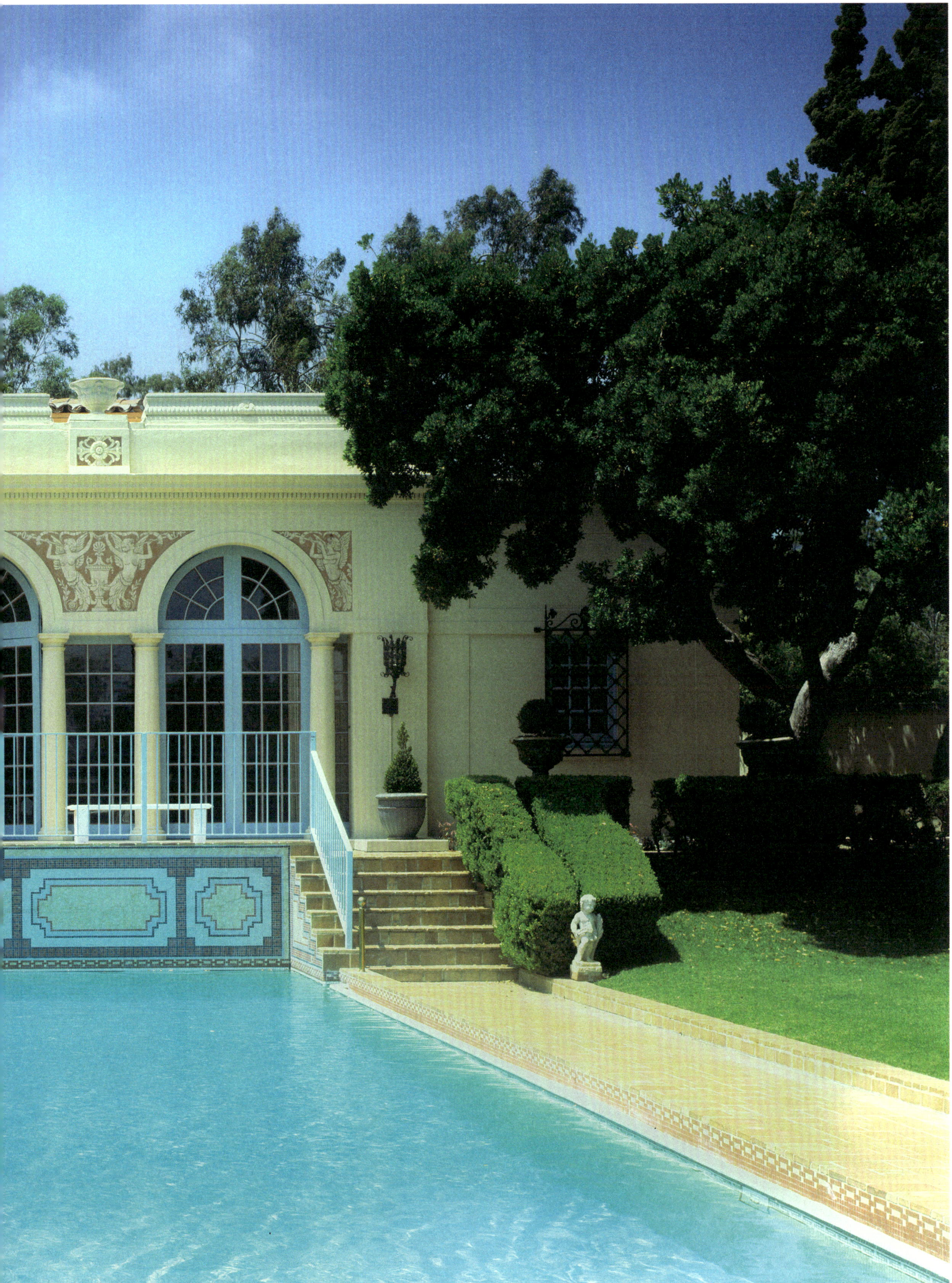

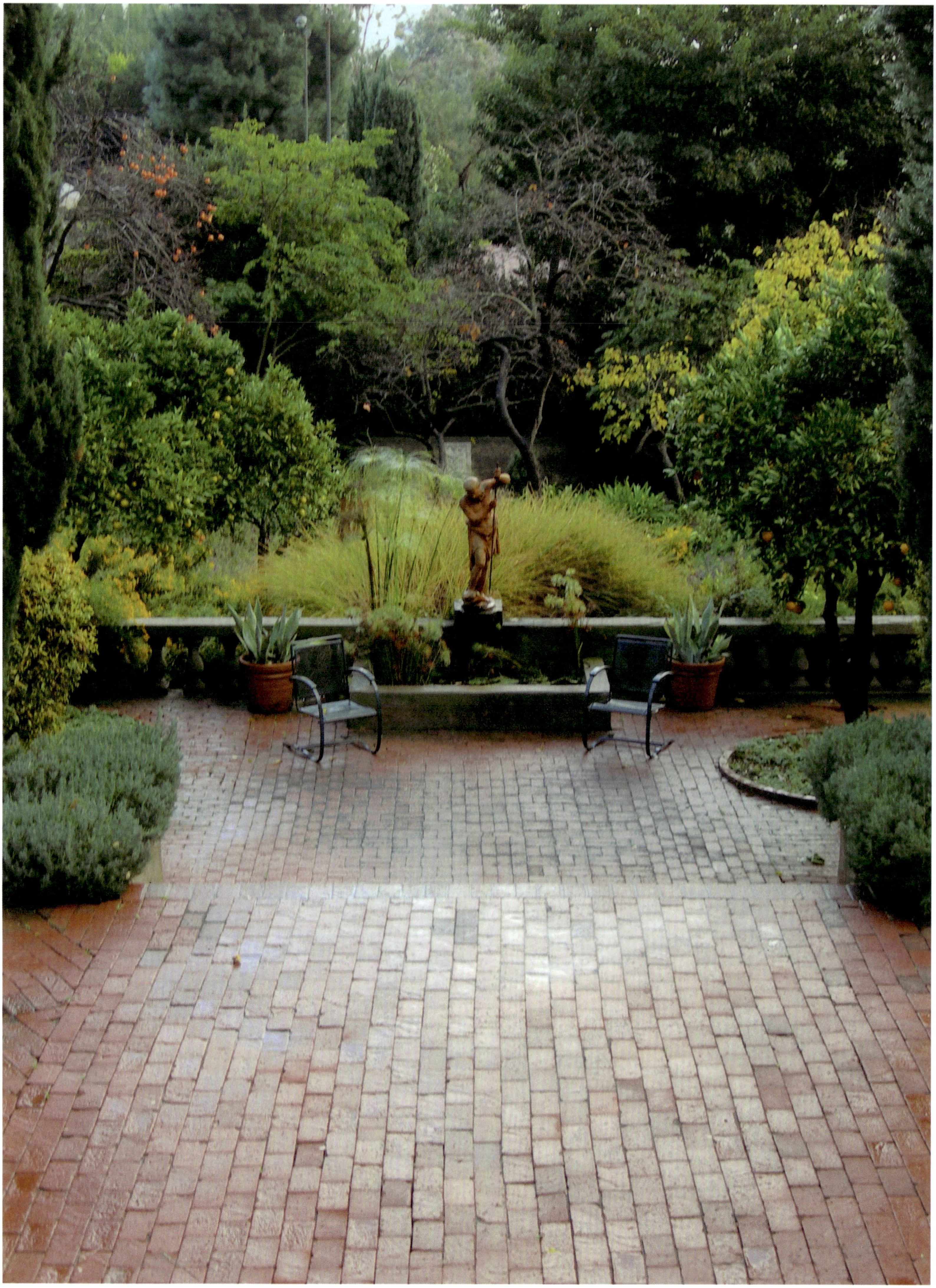

THE ITALIAN TERRACE GARDEN

The Italian Terrace Garden was laid out some time after Harry Robinson had passed away. This garden was designed primarily with the assistance of Charles Curtis, Virginia's second majordomo, who oversaw the Robinson staff from 1939 to 1969. Curtis, an architect trained in London, was involved with the gardens and house additions, as well as carrying out his other duties. The Italian Terrace Garden contains an eclectic assortment of plants beloved by Virginia. Below the Musical Stairs, there is a collection of camellias and azaleas. When Virginia was about to turn eighty years old, her friends asked her what she might like for her birthday. She replied that she wanted any gift that cost less than a "buck." She got eighty one-gallon azaleas for her birthday.

The Maidenhair tree at the top of the Italian Terrace Garden had great appeal for Virginia. A handsome, upright tree with exceptional autumn color, this deciduous tree was planted in the 1930s. Growing below Virginia's dressing room window is another historically significant plant, a night-blooming Organ Pipe cactus now some twenty feet tall. Arabella and Henry Huntington harvested a foot-long cutting from their famous garden in San Marino as a gift for Virginia.

The Italian Terrace Garden is laid out in classical style, nearly bilaterally symmetrical with a sight line down the middle. One enters off the Great Lawn and walks through an allee of Southern Magnolia trees. Beyond the canopy of these trees, the garden opens up with a spectacular vista to the five terraced areas below. The garden features start on the first terrace with the Three Frog Fountain and Musical Stairs. Virginia named this water feature with rills (stair treads) and runnels (stair risers) the "Musical Stairs" because the sound of the falling water created a soothing melody. As one descends the stairs, the sound is naturally amplified by the wall at the bottom.

Next down the slope is the Citrus Terrace, which includes a cave-like water feature called the Grotto, with soft sounds of falling water from its ceiling. After descending the center stairway from this terrace to the next, one arrives on the Lion Terrace. On either side of the stairway are lion statues. Along with the statue of Neptune below, they were imported from Florence, Italy, and were already a century old when they arrived on the property in the 1930s.

On the next terrace down, the statue of Neptune, the Roman god of the sea, stands timelessly guarding his aquatic garden. On the final terrace, at the lowest level of the garden, stands the three-tiered Italian fountain.

Noticeably, some of these garden features are not perfectly aligned on the garden's central axis, as would be dictated by the tradition of classical gardens. When asked about this, Virginia replied, "Life is not linear or symmetrical; why should my garden be?" According to many of Virginia's friends, her style of gardening was not heavy handed, and she would allow nature to guide the fate of the garden before she would decide to intervene.

Autumn foliage provides a spectacular backdrop for the Neptune Terrace.

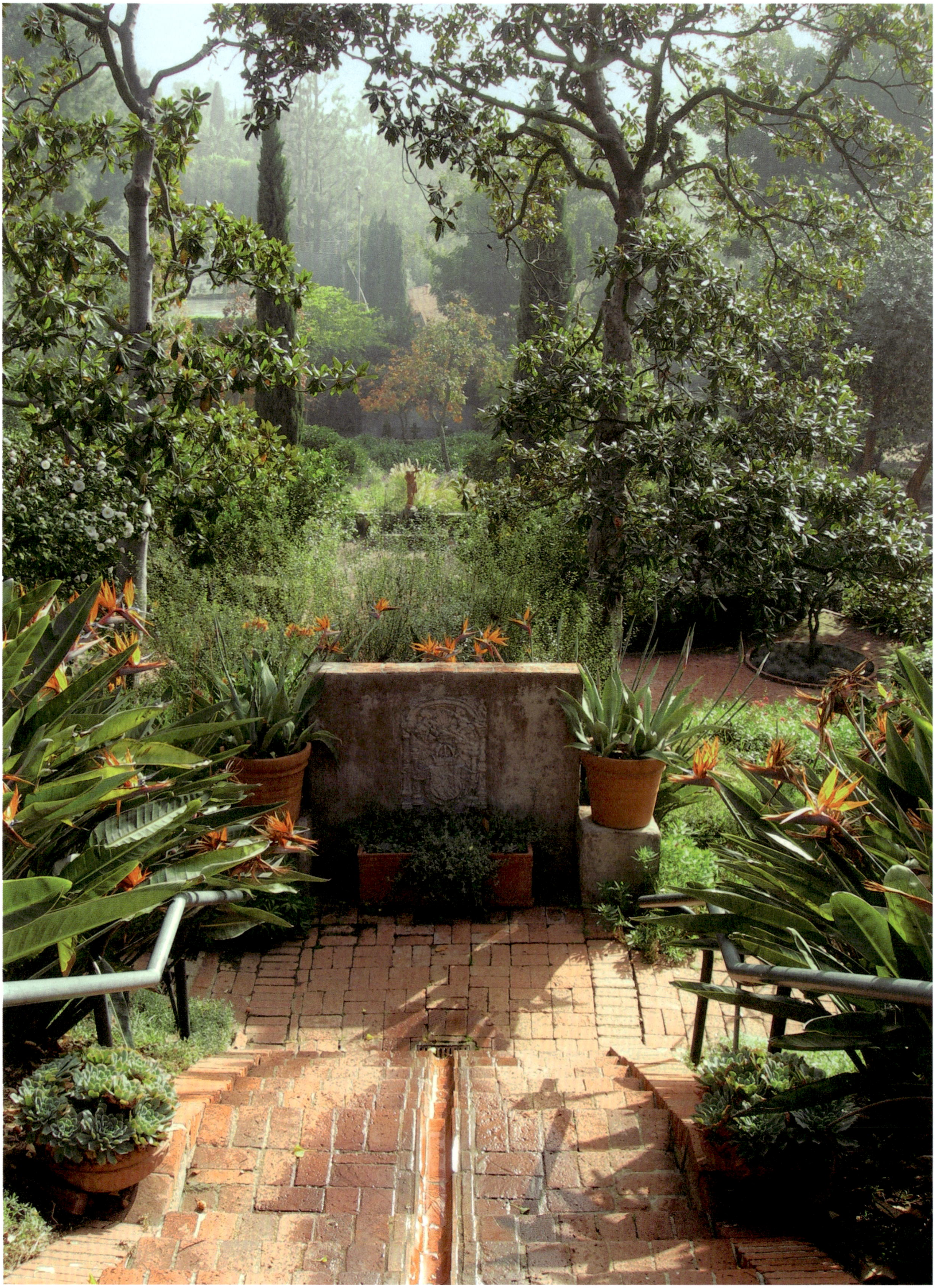

From her dressing room in the main house Virginia had a magnificent view of the Italian Terrace Garden. In February, the smell of citrus trees permeated this room and most of the rest of the house. The largest tree in the garden, the Coral tree, with its coral-shaped orange flowers, would be in full bloom starting in March. When she looked to the horizon in late afternoon, she would be able to see swaying palm trees framing the view to the island of Catalina, side-lit by the setting sun. This view, that fragrance and her closeness to the gardens, Virginia proclaimed, were what maintained her health and kept her young.

One attribute of most gardeners is that they share their bounty, whether it is extra produce, seeds, or actual cuttings, with others. So when the City of Los Angeles asked Virginia for cuttings from her Coral tree, she said yes without hesitation. You can now find the progeny of her tree growing along San Vicente Boulevard in West Los Angeles.

In front of a sea of fountain grass, Neptune stands with trident in hand.
OPPOSITE: *The sound of the falling water is amplified by the low wall at the bottom of the Musical Stairs.*

A WALK THROUGH THE GARDENS

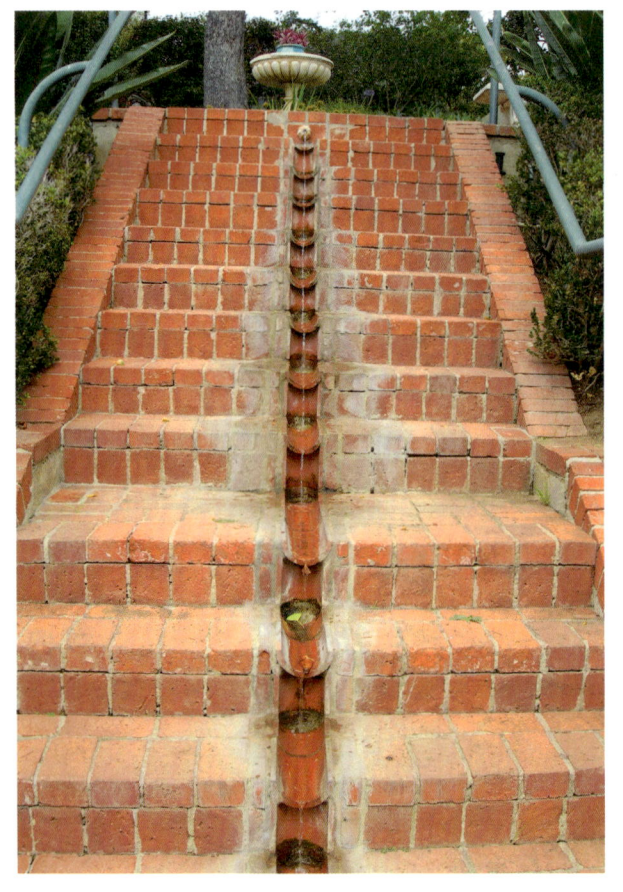

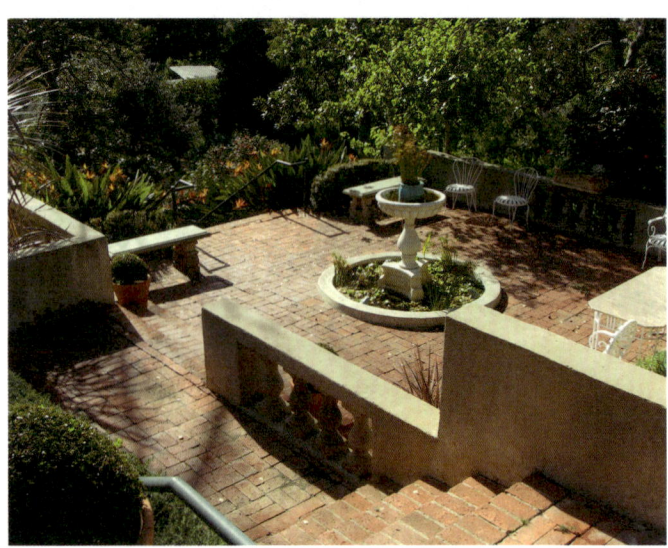

CLOCKWISE FROM TOP LEFT:

The Lion Terrace with the cave-like grotto between them

The giant Coral tree framed by two Italian Cypress trees

The Three Frog Fountain Terrace

The Musical Stairs

BEVERLY HILLS' FIRST ESTATE

CLOCKWISE FROM TOP LEFT:

Trunk of Coral tree with olive jar

Italian marble font with Kolanchoe plant

Three-Tiered Italian Fountain with moss encrusted brick terrace

Pipe Organ cactus, a gift from Henry and Arabella Huntington of San Marino, California

{79}

🌿 A WALK THROUGH THE GARDENS

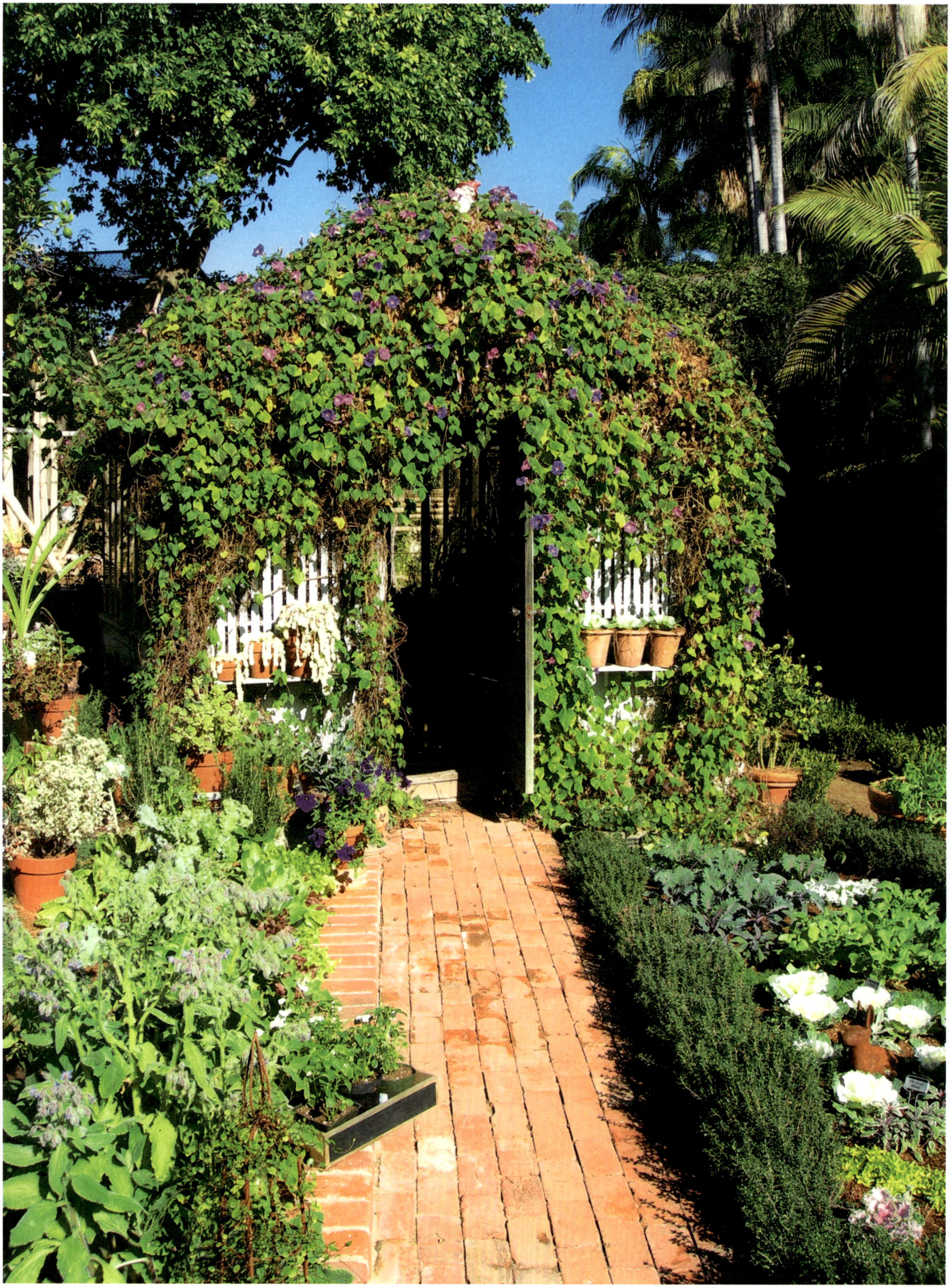

THE KITCHEN TERRACE AND THE ORCHID GREENHOUSE

After crossing the back terrace of the house, one can walk along the northeast extension of the Residence until one finds the gateway through the wall, which leads to the Kitchen Terrace. The Terrace connects the laundry room, male and female staff quarters, and kitchen. It allows access to the Orchid Greenhouse and Kitchen Garden as well as to the lower garage where the Robinsons' three Duesenbergs were housed.

The whole of this area was utilitarian by design and used only by the staff. Virginia never used the kitchen entrance of the Main Residence, even when her garden walks were suddenly cut short by rain. If her majordomo suggested they take a shortcut through the kitchen, she would always decline, saying it wouldn't be proper to disturb the kitchen staff.

On the Kitchen Terrace are two very old Sweet Olive shrubs, planted on either side of the steps leading down from the Great Lawn. They have small flowers, barely noticeable, but they provide an enormous perfume capable of stopping people passing by in their tracks to investigate its source. The scent is musk-like, similar to a gardenia.

The narrow passage alongside the laundry room leads to the Kitchen Garden and Orchid Greenhouse. A large Bay Laurel shrub grows there. Trained on the laundry room wall is a fragrant pink climbing rose, called "Cecile Brunner," as well as a yellow variegated pointed ivy, which gives a rich textural effect to the vertical surface.

The Orchid Greenhouse was a gift from composer Les Baxter. Originally, it was sited on the roof of the Pool Pavilion, but a year in that spot proved that location impractical and it was moved. As the greenhouse name implies, it produces orchids used for display in the Main Residence and Pool Pavilion.

Behind the Orchid Greenhouse is the monkey cage, which initially contained three monkeys. A white Sapote tree from central Mexico still grows over the cage. This tree supplied the monkeys with supplemental fruit through the summer months. Many party guests would find time to visit the comical monkeys, though one unfortunate guest lost her wig to a monkey. Today, the monkey cage is occupied by less mischievous topiary monkeys.

The Kitchen Garden was created by a fifteen-foot concrete retaining wall with the driveway below. As they are today, the vegetable beds were changed out with seasonal crops. Mainstays in the Kitchen Garden were French Sorrel, an herb called Salad Burnet, various mints and thymes, cilantro, and sweet basil. Adjacent to the two lemon trees, tomatoes were regularly planted.

Barbara Bonifield Himes recalled that the very first time she experienced "the thrill" of chewing on a spearmint leaf was in her Aunt Gigi's garden. "I was very young, and thus amazed that this was the source of spearmint flavor."

The Orchid Greenhouse covered with purple morning glory vine

On the east side of the Main Residence was an experimental garden, which later was replaced by the majestic Palm Forest.

CLOCKWISE FROM TOP LEFT:

Narrow pathway leads to the Orchid Greenhouse and Kitchen Garden

The Kitchen Terrace with ivy-covered laundry room

The monkey cage today with topiary monkeys

Driveway to porte cochere under male staff quarters

A WALK THROUGH THE GARDENS

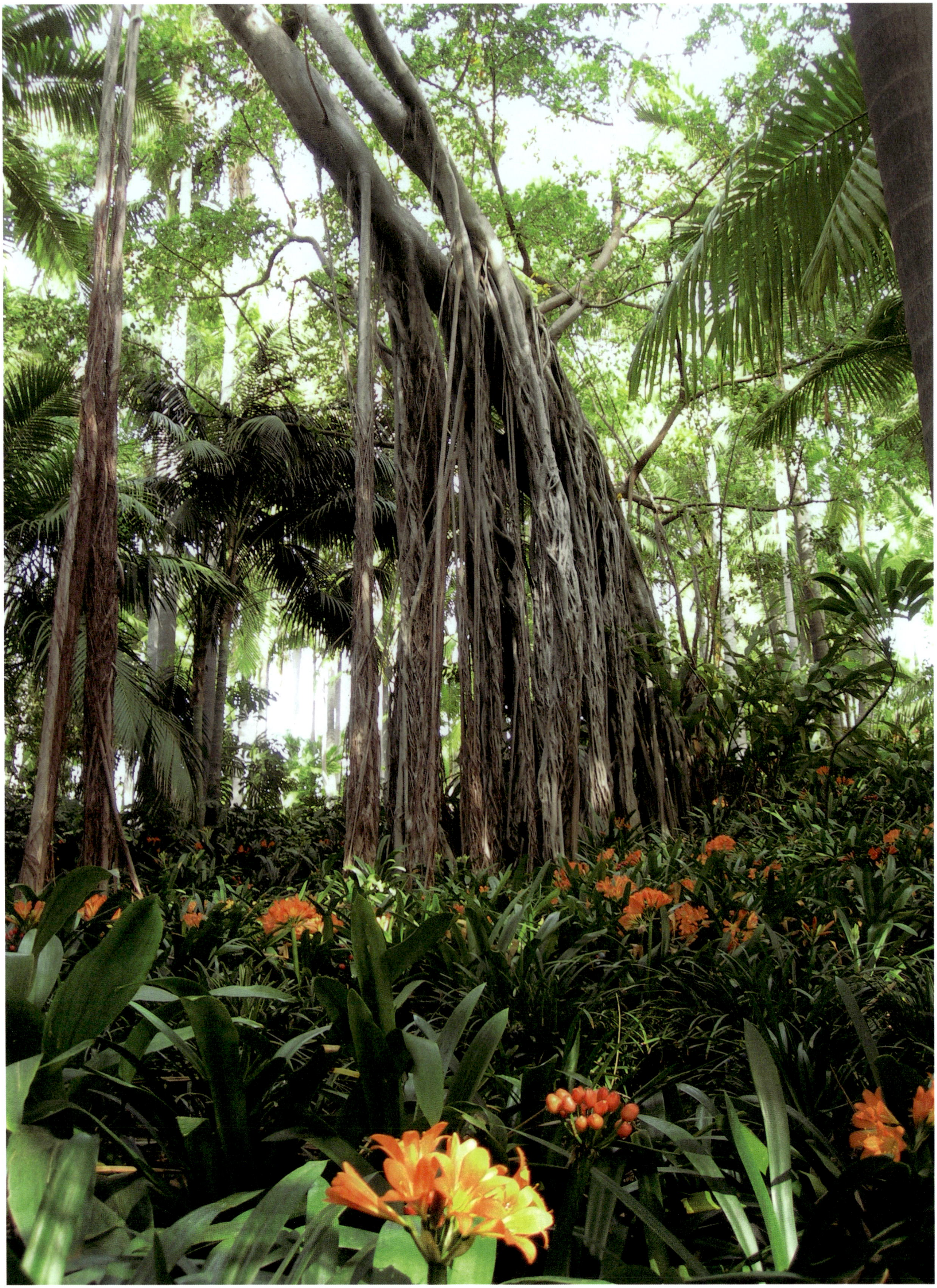

THE PALM FOREST

In the early 1920s, the garden now called the Palm Forest was laid out with brick and decomposed granite walkways. This roughly two-acre area was planted with citrus and other Mediterranean plants. Over the next few years, the garden slowly declined, primarily due to heavy, poorly drained soils. As an east slope, it receives the cooler morning sun and is shaded by early afternoon, due to the topography. Therefore, this area remains moist for prolonged periods of time. These conditions were not conducive to growing the selected plants from Mediterranean regions of the world.

In the mid-1920s, the Robinsons consulted with Charles Gibbs Adams, a renowned landscape architect. Since this area was naturally wet and with available supplies of portable water from the Owens Valley, he suggested planting tropical plants. The Robinsons took Mr. Adams' advice and transformed this area into the Tropical Forest. It was planted with hundreds of King Palms from Queensland, Australia. It is unclear if the palms were started from small plants or from seed. The Robinsons started many of their plants from seed; so it is plausible they purchased seeds. This area mimicked the native conditions of Queensland so well that after the trees matured, they produced seed of their own and populated the hillside. Today the Palm Forest has the largest stand of King Palms outside of Australia. The palms tower above the visitor by some sixty feet.

Planted in mass, the Kaffir lily flower grows across the forest floor. Its flowers begin to appear in early March and finish in late May. During this period, the tangerine trumpet-shaped flower is a bright beacon of color. Other plants in the shade of the King Palms include the Lady Palm and Bamboo Palm. Harry was keen on growing ferns and was recognized as a serious fern collector and grower; he amassed a significant collection on his Beverly Hills estate. Today, only a remnant of his fern collection remains in the Palm Forest.

The most exotic and interesting specimen tree in this garden is the Walking Banyan Fig tree. This eighty-foot-tall tree resembles a giraffe with its head stretched to the sky, reaching for the sunlight above its competitors, the King Palms. It has adapted to compete with other vegetation by producing aerial and prop-roots. The aerial roots absorb the nutrients washing out of the canopy before they ever reach the ground where other plants wait to suck them up. The prop roots look like the legs of a giraffe and function to steady and support large tree limbs.

Further along the shady path through the Palm Forest is the Palm Terrace with a rectangular pond and water feature. This area is open to the sky, and the dominating feature is a one-hundred-year old Blue Gum Eucalyptus tree. A receipt from 1911 indicated the Robinsons purchased one hundred Blue Gum Eucalyptus trees for one dollar each. They were planted initially to provide a wind break. As the gardens matured, all but one Eucalyptus was removed. The remaining one is the oldest plant on the estate.

The Walking Banyan Fig tree from Queensland, Australia, is under planted with Kaffir lily.

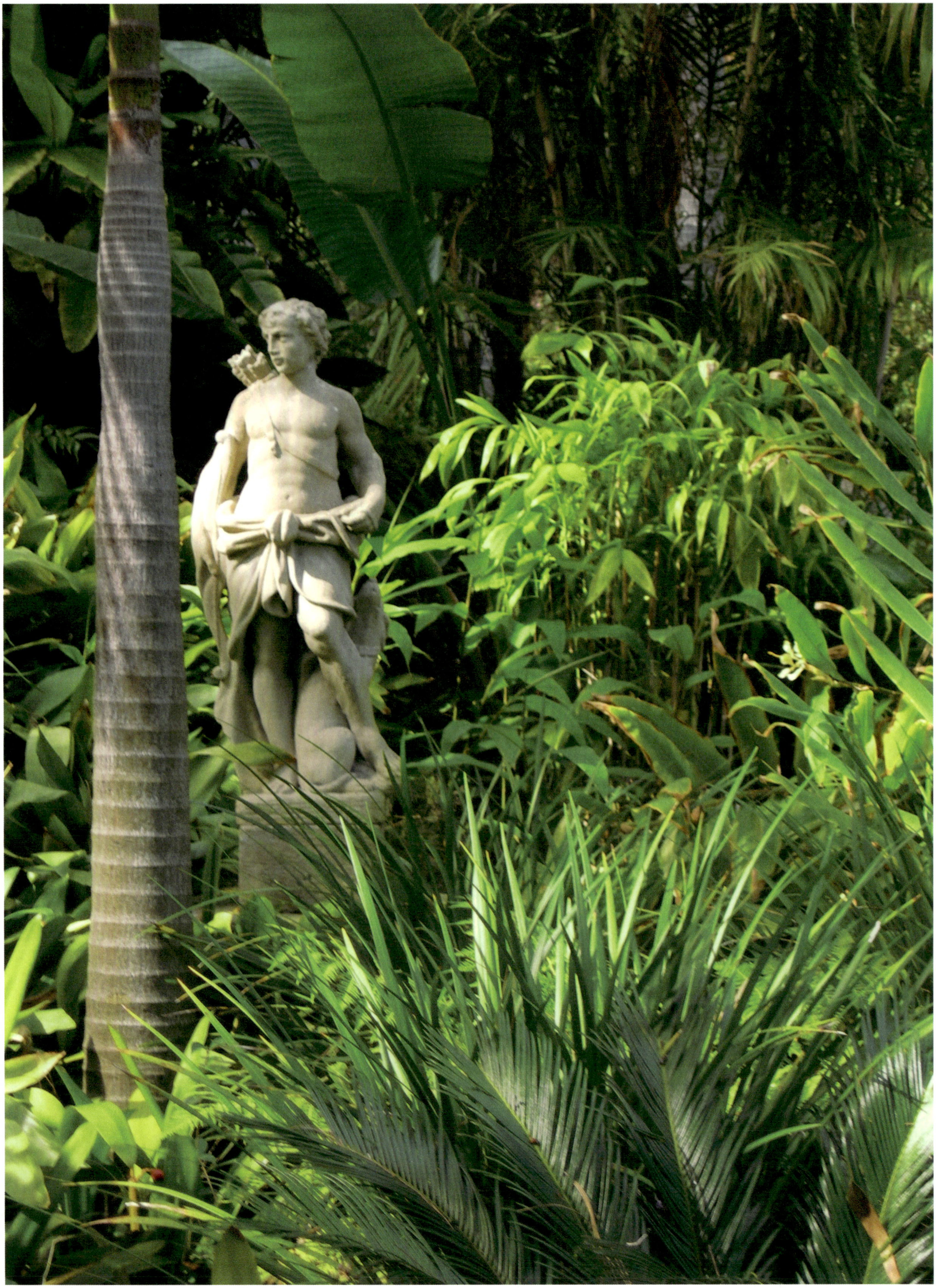

The Palm Terrace, which features a rectangular aquatic garden and runnel, carries water to the reservoir below.
OPPOSITE: *The Neoclassical statue of Cupid is surrounded by a myriad of plant textures in the Palm Forest.*

A WALK THROUGH THE GARDENS

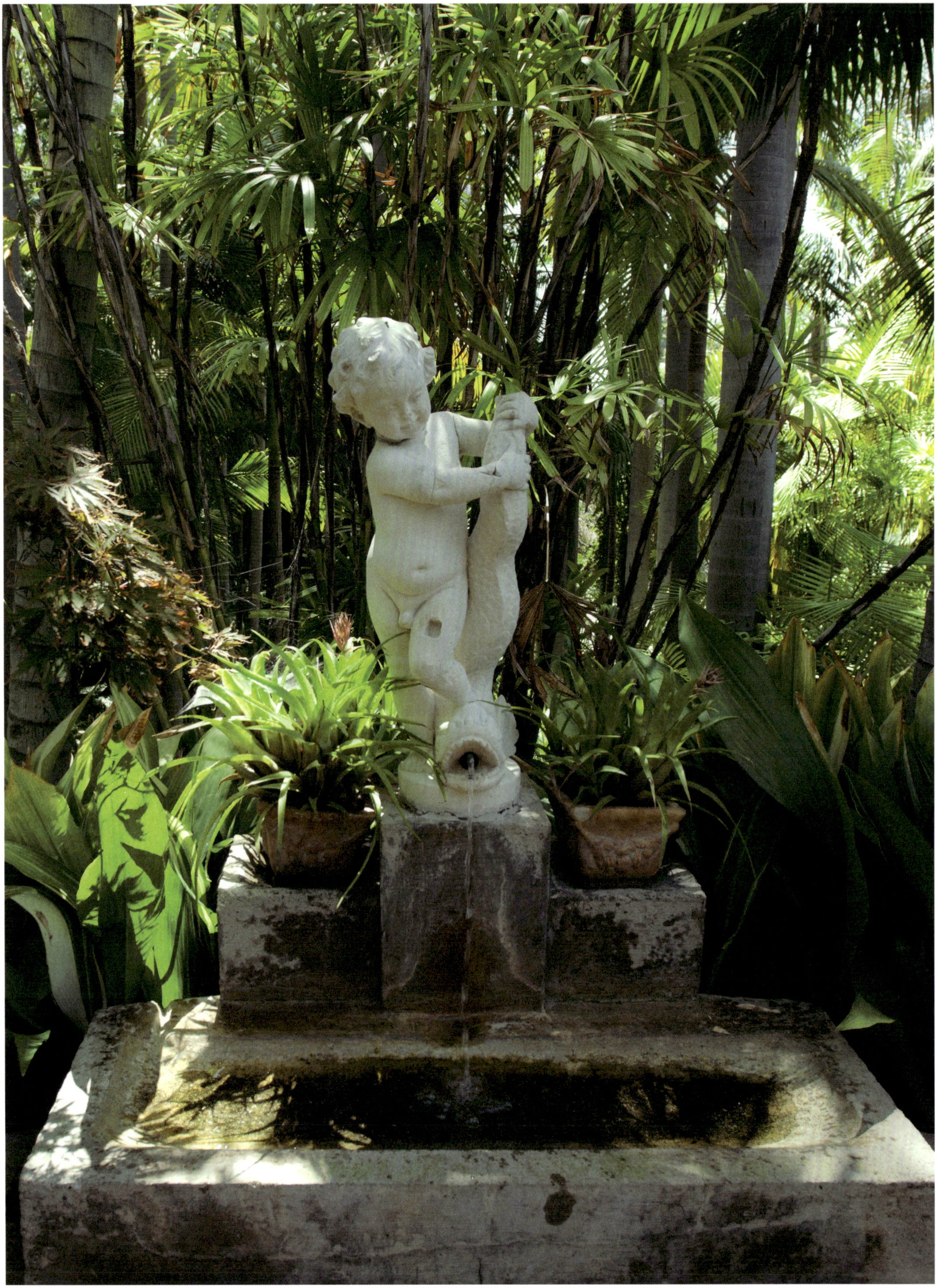

THE TENNIS COURT AND THE DISPLAY ROSE GARDEN

Virginia and Harry gained inspiration by touring gardens around the world. While traveling in South Africa, Virginia played tennis on a court she so admired that she recreated it on her own estate. From a cutting she brought back from her trip, she started the bougainvillea that blooms at the end of the court. She painted the walls of her court to match those she saw in South Africa.

On the tennis observation deck in the 1920s and 1930s it would be possible to see director's chairs filled with real directors, watching the game in progress. Jack and Ann Warner, George Cukor, and Charlie Chaplin were among the regular players. On Sundays the group usually played mixed doubles and, with mannerly deference to Virginia, commonly awarded her team the match. In the early years of the Robinsons' residency, a second tennis court made of turf for the gentleman to play on was located in the lower portion of the Italian Terrace Garden. The gentlemen would return to the upper tennis court to join the ladies for lunch, which was served smorgasbord style. Frequently after lunch guests would change into their bathing suits and stay for a swim.

Adjacent to the tennis court is the Display Rose Garden. It is planted with approximately two hundred hybrid tea roses, its flowers ranging in color from lightest pink to the deepest blood red. A hybrid tea rose with medium warm-pink flowers called "Eiffel Tower" was Virginia's favorite rose. She admired it not only because it was her favorite color pink, but also because of its intoxicating fragrance. This rose grows on the iron tower north of the tennis observation deck. It was introduced by Armstrong Nursery in 1963. Ivo Hadjiev regularly picked this rose for her, placing a single stem in a silver vase at her place setting in the dining room of the Main Residence.

Along the drive are two varieties of climbing roses, intertwined on five iron arches. "Sally Holmes" is a white five-petaled rose with a blush of pink in the middle. It starts to bloom in mid-April and finishes in early June. "Altissimo" is a bright red five-petaled rose. It starts to bloom in early May, finishing in early July. The total length of the display is approximately twelve weeks due to their overlapping bloom times.

As the name of the garden implies, these roses are for display, not for bouquets. Roses used in floral arrangements at the galas and other parties were collected from the Cutting Rose Garden. The Cutting Rose Garden is located on a hillside east of the tennis court and contains about four hundred roses. The roses in this garden are not tightly orchestrated by color. In fact, all the colors of the rainbow are represented. When viewing this garden, Virginia would declare, "nothing and no one can replicate the colors of nature."

The Cherub Fountain stands adjacent to the aviary.

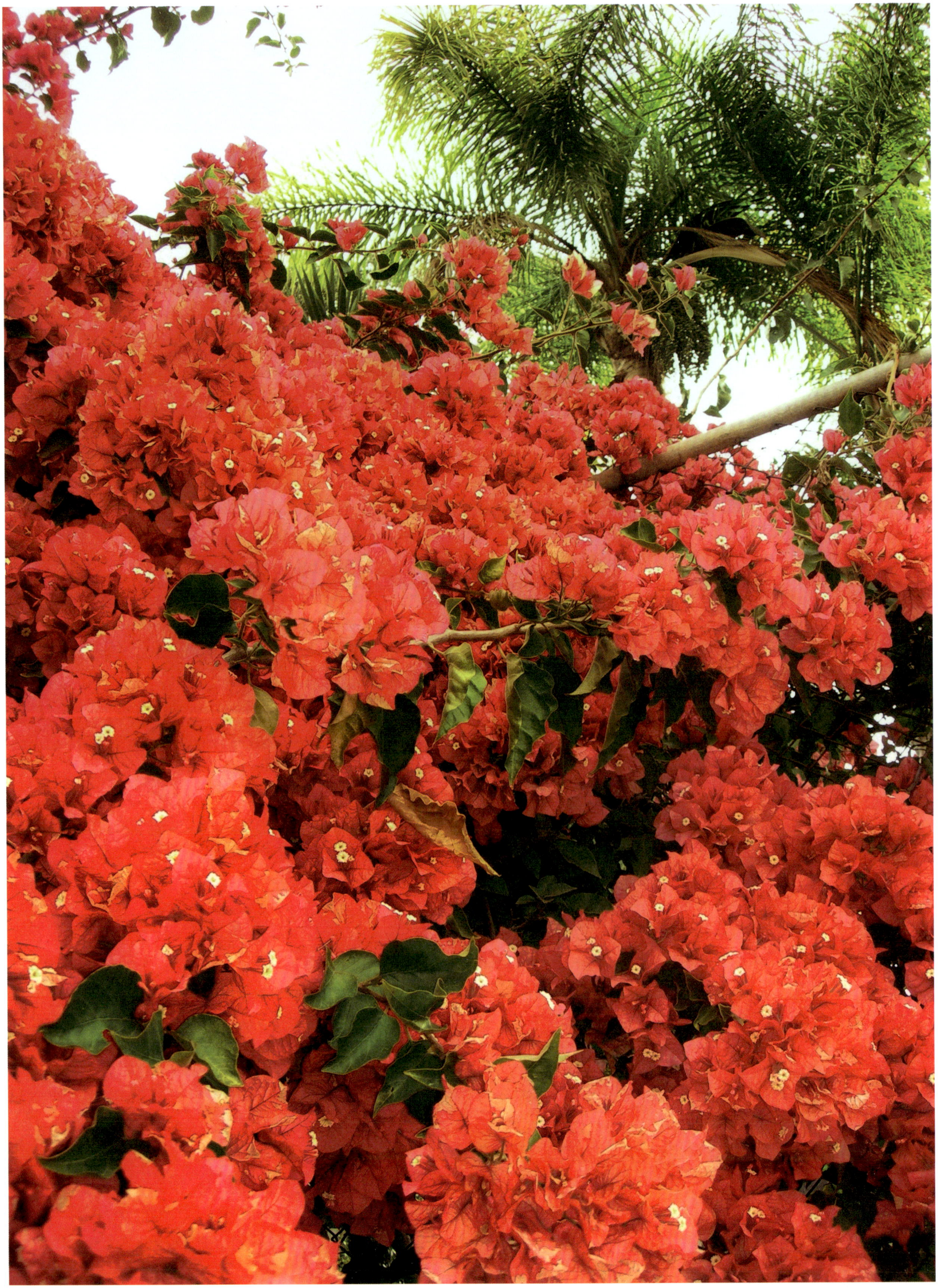

The bougainvillea covering the entire back wall of the Tennis Court blooms nearly year-round. It was propagated from a cutting made by Virginia while traveling in South Africa.

A white five-petaled rose called "Sally Holmes" grows on a series of arches at the rear of the Display Rose Garden.

OPPOSITE: *A close-up of the bougainvillea reveals its flowers are actually white while the pink modified leaves (bract) provide the stunning color of this vine.*

A WALK THROUGH THE GARDENS

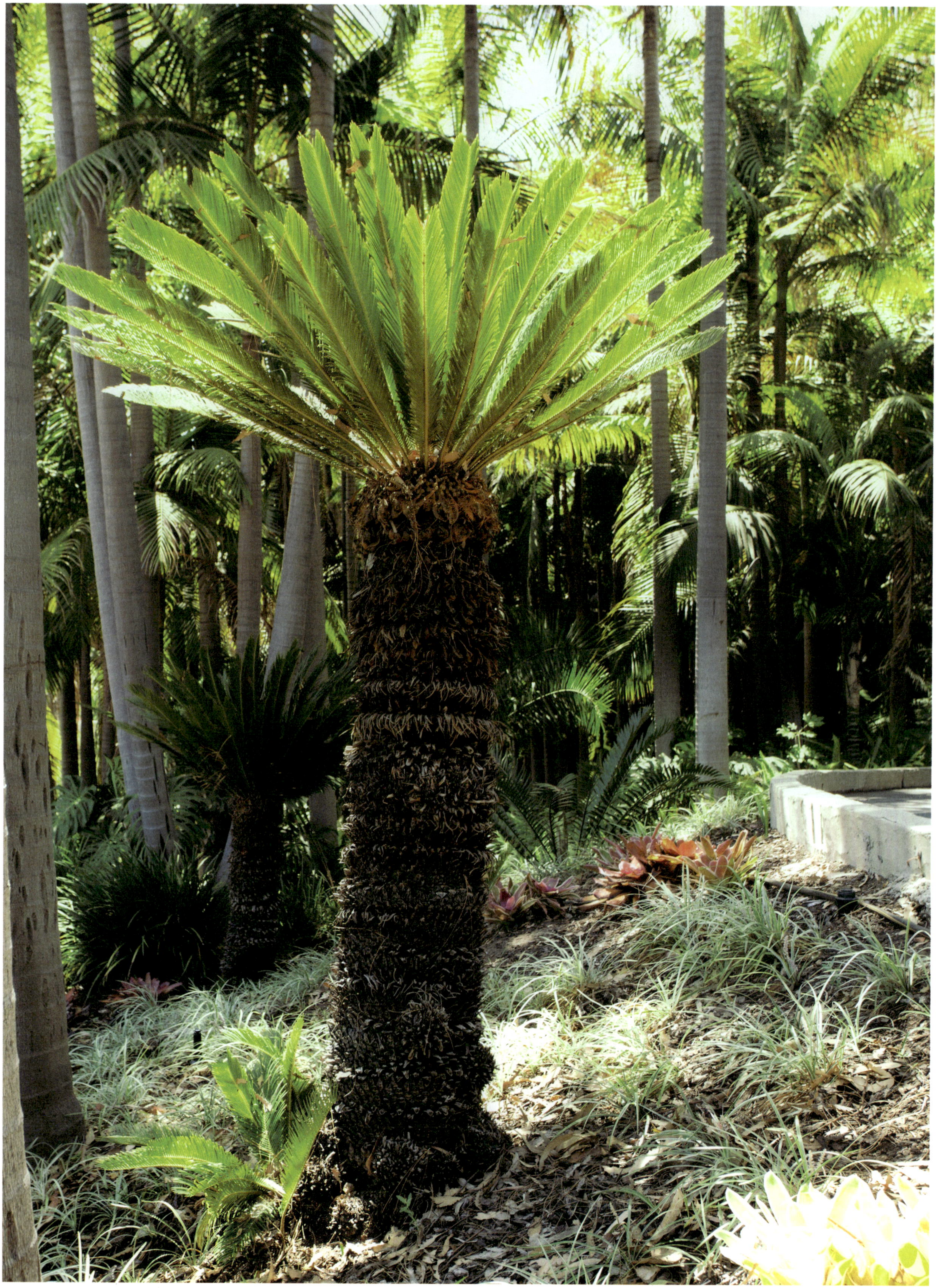

THE VIRGINIA ROBINSON GARDENS TODAY

Virginia Robinson generously donated her estate to the County of Los Angeles in 1977. As she intended, the estate is currently operated as a garden and museum for the public to enjoy. The underlying goals are to further the public's appreciation and knowledge of horticulture along with the interpretation and preservation of this cultural artifact.

The property is listed on The National Register of Historic Places by the United States Department of Interior. Consequently, all restoration of the property is completed following the Department's rules and regulations for listed historic properties. The collections policies set forth by the American Association of Museums are adhered to when restoring artifacts in the collections.

The County collaborates with the Friends of Robinson Gardens, a support organization started in 1982, to secure the necessary funding to restore and preserve the estate. Interior and exterior restoration programs continue to touch most aspects of the estate in order to maintain and restore the Virginia Robinson Gardens' grandeur.

On a regular basis, docents provide a living interpretation of the estate. During a ninety minute walking tour, docents give a look back at an early twentieth century lifestyle—a bygone era. In addition, the gardens offer ongoing educational programs related to topics of historical interest and botanical subjects as well as art classes. The Friends' website lists historical information as well as future programs and other upcoming events at www.robinsongardens.org.

In May of each year, the Friends sponsor a fundraiser to help support the Virginia Robinson Gardens. This event has occurred annually since 1985. It promotes both floral design and fine gardening while featuring the Gardens and privately owned gardens that are open to ticket holders only on that day. Another fundraiser takes place on one special evening of the year when the Great Lawn is transformed into a magical wonderland reminiscent of the Robinsons' era. On that evening the patrons of the Garden are celebrated at a dinner and dance for their dedication and financial support of the Virginia Robinson Gardens.

There are many opportunities to get involved with the Virginia Robinson Gardens as a volunteer. In fact, each year nine thousand hours are volunteered at the Virginia Robinson Gardens. Please consider joining the many volunteers devoted to the noble cause of preserving an important part of our regional and national history.

Ancient Sago Palms grow above the Palm Terrace.

PAGE 96: *The large Blue Gum Eucalyptus tree (center) is the oldest plant on the estate.*

VIRGINIA ROBINSON GARDENS HISTORICAL PLANT LIST COMPILED MARCH 2011

The following plants were planted by Harry and Virginia Robinson during their residency from 1911 until 1977 and still grow on the Robinson estate today.

THE FRONT GARDEN

COMMON NAME	BOTANICAL NAME
English Boxwood	*Buxus sempervirens*
Gold Medallion Tree	*Cassia leptophylla*
Organ Pipe Catus	*Cereus peruviannus*
Paradise Palm	*Howea forsteriana*
Jacaranda	*Jacaranda mimosifolia*
Bay Laurel Hedge	*Laurus nobilis*
Himalayan Laurel	*Cocculus Laurifolius*
Southern Magnolia	*Magnolia grandiflora*
Tulip Magnolia	*Magnolia x soulangeana*
Wisteria Vine	*Wisteria sinensis*

THE GREAT LAWN

COMMON NAME	BOTANICAL NAME
Lily-of-the-Nile	*Agapanthus africanus*
Strawberry Tree	*Arbutus unedo*
English Boxwood	*Buxus sempervirens*
Red Powder Puff Tree	*Calliandra haematocephala*
Italian Cypress Tree	*Cupressus sempervirens*
Prickly Cycad	*Encephalartos altensteinii*
Cockspur Coral Tree	*Erythrina crista-galli*
Iochroma	*Iochroma cyaneum*
Hollywood Juniper	*Juniperus c. 'Torulosa'*
Kikuyu Grass	*Kikuyu spp.*
Boston Ivy	*Parthenocissus quinquefolia*
Joseph's Coat Rose	*Rosa spp.*
Madagascar Jasmine	*Stephanotis floribunda*
Orange Honeysuckle	*Tecoma capensis*
Yellow Honeysuckle	*Tecoma capensis 'Aurea'*

THE KITCHEN GARDEN

COMMON NAME	BOTANICAL NAME
Sapote Tree	*Casimiroa edulis*
Lemon Trees	*Citrus limon 'Eureka'*
Creeping Fig	*Ficus pumila*
Pointed Ivy	*Hedera helix*
Bay Laurel Tree	*Laurus nobilis*
Sweet Olive (Hedge)	*Osmanthus fragrans*
Boston Ivy	*Parthenocissus quinquefolia*

THE TENNIS COURT

COMMON NAME	BOTANICAL NAME
Pink Bougainvillea	*Bougainvillea spp.*
Blood Trumpet Vine	*Distictis buccinatoria*

THE CUT GARDEN

COMMON NAME	BOTANICAL NAME
Blue Agave	*Agave americana*
Floss Silk Tree	*Chorisia speciosa*

THE ITALIAN TERRACE GARDEN

COMMON NAME	BOTANICAL NAME
Blue Elderberry Tree	*Sambucus mexicana*
Lily-of-the-Nile	*Agapanthus africanus*
Strawberry Trees	*Arbutus unedo*
Flame Tree	*Brachychiton acerifolius*
Bird of Paradise	*Strelitzia reginae*
Camellia (various)	*Camellia spp.*
Deodar Cedar	*Cedrus deodara*
Citrus (various)	*Citrus spp.*
Kaffir Lily	*Clivia miniata*
Crinum Lily	*Crinum spp.*
Montbretia	*Crocosmia X crocosmiiflora*
Italian Cypress Trees	*Cupressus sempervirens*
Persimmon Trees	*Diospyros kaki*
Loquat Trees	*Eriobotrya japonica*
Coral Trees	*Erythrina caffra*
Pineapple Guavas	*Feijoa sellowiana*
African Gardenia	*Gardenia thunbergia*
Maidenhair Tree	*Ginkgo biloba*
White Hibiscus	*Hibiscus spp.*
California Walnut	*Juglans californica*
Bay Laurel (Hedge)	*Laurus nobilis*
Japanese Honeysuckle	*Lonicera japonica*
Apple Trees	*Malus spp.*
Southern Magnolia Trees	*Magnolia grandiflora*
Red Mulberry Trees	*Morus rubra*
African Boxwood (Hedge)	*Myrsine africana*
Olive Trees	*Olea europaea*
Avocado Trees	*Persea americana*
Stone Fruit Trees	*Prunus spp.*
Pomegranate (Hedge)	*Punica granatum*
Azaleas (Various)	*Rhododendron spp.*
Robinia Tree	*Robinia pseudoacacia 'Frisia'*
Giant Bird of Paradise	*Strelizia nicolai*
Montezuma Cyprus	*Taxodium mucronatum*
Society Garlic	*Tulbaghia violacea*
Sweet Violet	*Viola odorata*
New Zealand Chaste Tree	*Vitex agnus-castus*

THE PALM FOREST

COMMON NAME	BOTANICAL NAME
Agave	*Agave attenuata*
King Palm Trees	*Archontophoenix cunninghamiana*
Cast Iron Plant	*Aspidistra elatior*
Pindo Palm	*Butia capitata*
Bismarkia Palm	*Bismarkia nobilis*
Bottlebrush Tree	*Callistemon citrinus*
Fish Tail Palm	*Caryota mitis*
Fish Tail Wine Palm	*Caryota urens*
Bamboo Palm	*Chamaedorea elegans*
Mediterranean Fan Palm	*Chamaerops humilis*
Fortnight Lily	*Dietes iridioides*
Dianella	*Dianella tasmanica*
Kaffir Lily	*Clivia miniata*
Ti Plant	*Cordyline terminalis*
Holly Fern	*Cyrtominum falcatum*
Blue Gum Eucalyptus	*Eucalyptus globulust*
Morton Bay Fig	*Ficus macrophylla*
Indian Fig	*Ficus oligodon*
Banyan Fig Tree	*Ficus rubigninosa*
Flowering Ginger	*Hedychium spp.*
Swiss Cheese Plant	*Monstera friedrichsthalii*
Banana Tree	*Musa x paradisiaca*
Sword Fern	*Nephrolepis exaltata*
Date Palm	*Phoenix canariensis*
Giant Timber Bamboo	*Phyllostachys bambusoides*
Lady Palm	*Rhapis excelsa*
Parlor Palm	*Rhapis humilis*
Leather Fern	*Rumohra adiantiformis*
Giant Bird of Paradise	*Strelizia nicolai*
Queen Palm	*Syagrus romanzoffianum*
English Yew	*Taxus baccata*
Windmill Palm	*Trachycarpus fortunei*
California Fan Palm	*Washingtonia filifera*

POOL PAVILION

MAIN RESIDENCE

MALE STAFF QUARTERS

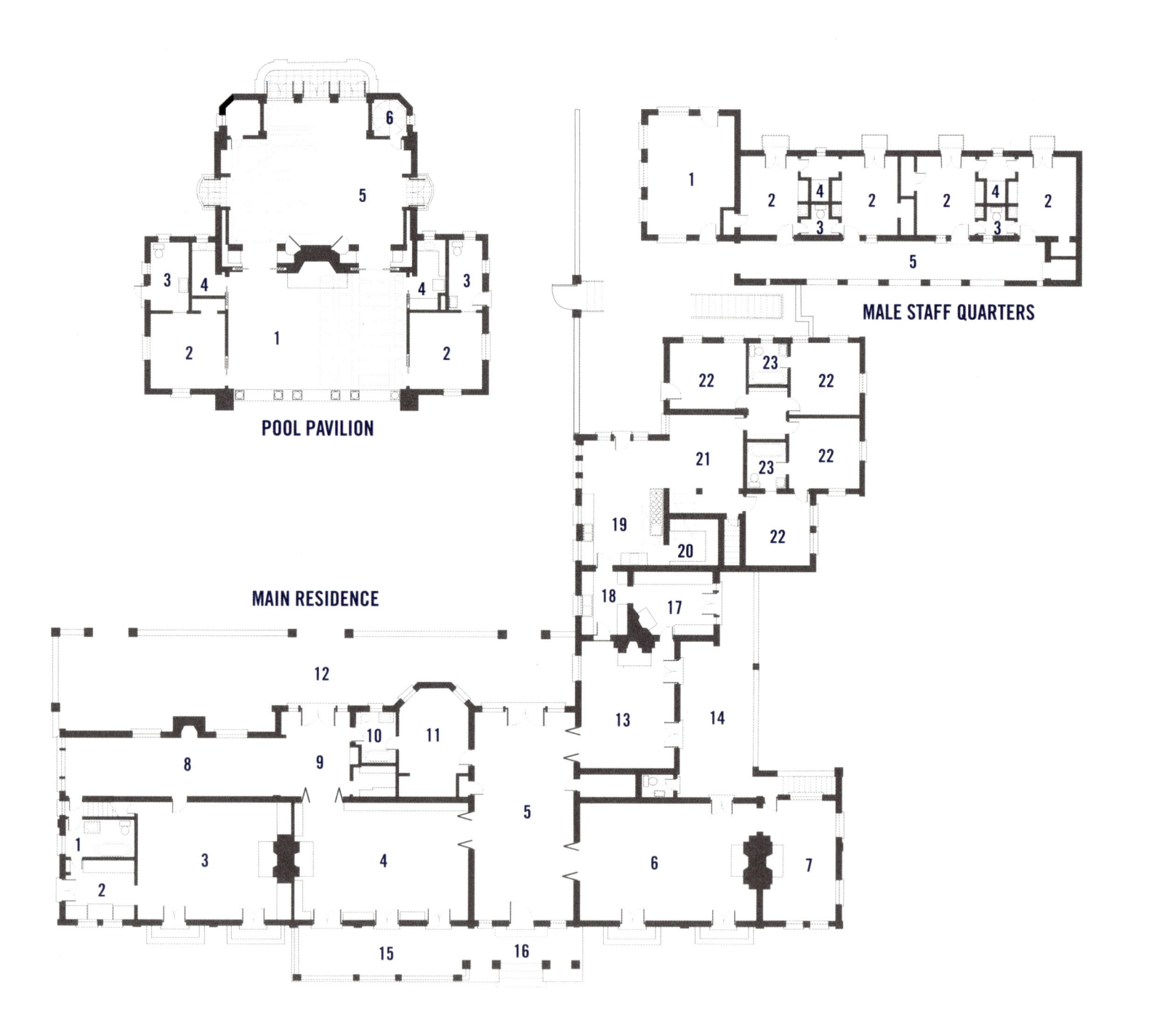

POOL PAVILION LEDGER
1. Solarium
2. Guest Room
3. Guest Bathroom
4. Kitchenette
5. Billiard Room
6. Spiral Staircase to Card Room

MALE STAFF QUARTERS LEDGER
1. Laundry Room
2. Bedroom
3. Toilet
4. Showers
5. Loggia

MAIN RESIDENCE LEDGER
1. Master Bath
2. Dressing Room
3. Master Bedroom
4. Library
5. Entry Hall
6. Golden Salon
7. Morning Room
8. Gallery
9. Gallery Entry
10. Guest Bathroom
11. Guest Bedroom
12. Back Terrazzo Terrace
13. Dining Room
14. Loggia
15. Front Porch
16. Front Entry
17. Majordomo's office
18. Butler's Pantry
19. Kitchen
20. Pantry
21. Staff Break Area
22. Female Staff Bedrooms
23. Female Staff Bathrooms